MEDIA, FEMINISM, CULTURAL STUDIES

Stepping Forward: Essays, Lectures and Interviews
by Wolfgang Iser

Wild Zones: Pornography, Art and Feminism
by Kelly Ives

Global Media Warning: Explorations of Radio, Television and the Press
by Oliver Whitehorne

'Cosmo Woman': The World of Women's Magazines
by Oliver Whitehorne

Andrea Dworkin
by Jeremy Mark Robinson

Cixous, Irigaray, Kristeva: The Jouissance of French Feminism
by Kelly Ives

Sex in Art: Pornography and Pleasure in Painting and Sculpture
by Cassidy Hughes

*The Erotic Object: Sexuality in Sculpture
From Prehistory to the Present Day*
by Susan Quinnell

Women in Pop Music
by Helen Challis

Detonation Britain: Nuclear War in the UK
by Jeremy Mark Robinson

Luce Irigaray: Lips, Kissing, and the Politics of Sexual Difference
by Kelly Ives

Helene Cixous I Love You: The Jouissance of Writing
by Kelly Ives

The Poetry of Cinema
by John Madden

The Sacred Cinema of Andrei Tarkovsky
by Jeremy Mark Robinson

Disney Business, Disney Films, Disney Lands
by Daniel Cerruti

Feminism and Shakespeare
by B.D. Barnacle

Julia Kristeva

Julia Kristeva

Art, Love, Melancholy, Philosophy, Semiotics and Psychoanalysis

Kelly Ives

CRESCENT MOON

CRESCENT MOON PUBLISHING
P.O. Box 1312, Maidstone
Kent, ME14 5XU
Great Britain
www.crmoon.com

First published 1998. Second edition 2008. Third edition 2010.
Fourth edition 2013.
© Kelly Ives 1998, 2008, 2010, 2013.

Printed and bound in the U.S.A.
Set in Palatino 9 on 14pt.
Designed by Radiance Graphics.

British Library Cataloguing in Publication data

British Library Cataloguing in Publication data

Ives, Kelly
Julia Kristeva: art, love, melancholy, philosophy, semiotics and
psychoanalysis
1. Kristeva, Julia, 1941-
I. Title
194
759.13

ISBN-13 9781861714176 (Pbk)
ISBN-13 9781861714220 (Hbk)

CONTENTS

ABBREVIATIONS

JULIA KRISTEVA

K	*The Kristeva Reader*
DL	*Desire in Language*
R	*Revolution in Poetic Language*
TL	*Tales of Love*
PH	*Powers of Horror*
ACW	*About Chinese Women*
BS	*Black Sun*
SO	*Strangers to Ourselves*
QS	"A Question of Subjectivity"

LUCE IRIGARAY

I	*The Irigaray Reader*
Je	*Je, tu, nous*
S	*Speculum*
TD	*Thinking the Difference*
Sex	*This Sex Which Is Not One*
EM	"Ecce Mulier?", in P. Burgard
ML	*Marine Lover of Friedrich Nietzsche*

HÉLÈNE CIXOUS

C	*The Hélène Cixous Reader*
NBW	*The Newly Born Woman*
BP	*The Book of Promethea*
EHC	"An Exchange with Hélène Cixous", interview, in V. Conley,

1991
Con   "Conversations", in S. Sellers, 1988
EF   "Extreme Fidelity", in S. Sellers,1988
DJ   "Difficult Joys", in H. Wilcox, 1990

M   *New French Feminisms*, Marks & de Courtivron, eds

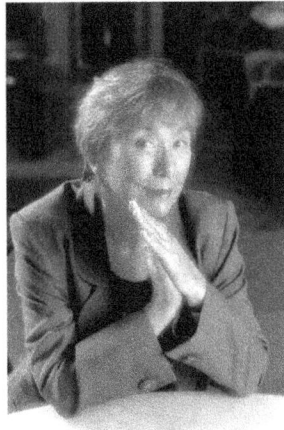

Julia Kristeva

PREFACE

This book is a poetic study of French feminist and philosopher Julia Kristeva. Part of this book appeared as a study of three French feminists, Hélène Cixous, Julia Kristeva and Luce Irigaray, who are called the 'holy trinity' of French feminism (D. Landry, 1993, 54). Before addressing Kristeva's work I survey some of the key elements of the feminist philosophy of Cixous, Irigaray and Kristeva. French feminism is often reduced to meaning the writings of this 'holy trio', while at other times it refers to criticism in the wake of Jacques Lacan, Jacques Derrida and Michel Foucault (these three male writers are sometimes seen as an equivalent of the Cixous-Irigaray-Kristeva trinity [J. Duran, 163]).

Some feminists are suspicious of calling Hélène Cixous, Luce Irigaray and Julia Kristeva 'radical': for Chris Weedon they are radical (Irigaray in particular [1987, 9]), but not for Stevi Jackson.[1] Does it matter? The works of Cixous, Irigaray and Kristeva have gone beyond such notions. With its mixture of male writers (Derrida, Lacan, Foucault) and certain female writers (Kristeva, Cixous, Irigaray, Monique Wittig):

The boundaries of 'French feminism' are thus strangely constructed: some men fall within its definition, as do women who do not call themselves feminists, but those who have always called themselves feminists are excluded.[2]

As feminists/ philosophers/ speakers/ poets, Hélène Cixous, Luce Irigaray and Julia Kristeva are extraordinarily enriching. Their writings are alive, and they are not limited to having one or two things to say. Rather, they say a lot, about a lot. Sometimes they write things that are outrageous, at other times they are incredibly, searingly poignant. They upset many feminists – their insistence on the body and biology, for instance, aggravates some theorists.

This book is a poetic, intuitive study, which may not satisfy some people, because I do not work my way carefully and slowly through each stage of Julia Kristeva's career or writings. I do not offer in-depth analyses of every idea in Kristeva's *œuvre*. Rather, I hope to convey some the inspiration and excitement that her work instils. Kristeva, perhaps the most thoughtful and sober of the Cixous-Irigaray-Kristeva trio, also upsets critics. In her *About Chinese Women*, for instance, Kristeva produced ideas about people in the Far East which some commentators found distasteful and simplistic. Her views were imperialist, and generalized – both in Kristeva's portrayal of the Western position, and in her depiction of the Chinese woman. The ethnocentrism of *Des Chinoises* is problematic.[3]

The big name cultural philosophers and critics, among whom Hélène Cixous, Luce Irigaray and Julia Kristeva are major players, publish in academic journals such as *Diacritics, Signs, Feminist Studies, Tel Quel, differences, Camera Obscura, Screen, Wide Angle, Yale French Journal, October, Social Text* and *Monthly Review*. French feminism has been made more widely available in anthologies such as *New French Feminism* (1981) and *French Feminist Thought* (1987). Before these appeared, however, few of the full-length works of French feminists had been translated into English. Only by about 1985 had much of the work of Cixous, Kristeva and Irigaray been translated into English (J. Duran, 177).

Further, the theorists themselves (such as Monique Wittig, Annie Leclerc, Cixous, Kristeva, Irigaray), do not class themselves as 'feminists', in the same way Anglo-American feminists do.

French feminism is part of a movement in criticism which exalts post-modernism via modernism. The 'classic' modernists are exalted by the 'classic' postmodernists: Gustave Flaubert by Roland Barthes, René Magritte by Michel Foucault, James Joyce and Antonin Artaud by Julia Kristeva, Stéphane Mallarmé and Antonin Artaud by Jacques Derrida, Jean Genet and Marcel Proust by Hélène Cixous.[4]

PART ONE

❁

FRENCH FEMINISM

I

⊞

INTRODUCTORY

JULIA KRISTEVA: BIOGRAPHY

Julia Kristeva was born in Bulgaria on June 24, 1941. Educated in part by French nuns, she was involved early on in her life with Communist Party youth organizations and children's groups. Since moving to Paris in the 1960s, Kristeva has risen in stature in intellectual circles so that she is now regarded as one of the most important thinkers of the contemporary era. Early on Kristeva was associated with the Parisian journal *Tel Quel*, and the *Tel Quel* group of writers and philosophers: Michel Foucault, Roland Barthes, Jacques Derrida, Jean-Louis Baudry, Jean Pierre Faye, Marcelin Pleynet, Jean Ricardou, Jacqueline Risset, Denis Roche, Pierre Rottenberg, Jean Thibaudeau and Philippe Sollers. Even in Bulgaria Kristeva was steeped in French culture. The Parisian intellectual life was seen as 'too French' by some (that being regarded as a bad thing). Kristeva herself was aware of the intensity of intellectual life in Paris:

> From the time of my arrival, I found, in this milieu, a distrustful and cold hospitality, that was nevertheless effective and dependable. A hospitality which has, moreover, never failed. Whatever the xenophobia, the antifeminism or the antisemitism of some, I maintain that French cultural life as I have come to know it has always been marked by a reserved but generous curiosity, one that is reticent but, everything considered, receptive to the nomad, the outlandish, the implant and the exogamous of all kinds. ("Mémoire", 42)

Roland Barthes wrote that Julia Kristeva 'changes the place of things... what she displaces is the *already-said*'.[2] Kristeva referred kindly to Barthes as 'the precursor and founder of modern literary studies' (DL, 93). Barthes was important in Kristeva's thought; from his work she developed the notion of the '*jouissance* of the text', the text as *jouissance*, especially as found in modern *avant garde* literature. In her *Le Texte du roman*, Kristeva referred to Georg Lukács, Ferdinand de Saussure, Roman Jakobson, Emile Benveniste, Naom Chomsky, Mikhail Bakhtin, Karl Marx and Friedrich Engels; in *Séméiotikè: Recherches pour une sémanalyse*, to Sigmund Freud and Jacques Lacan. Georges Bataille's philosophy, with its emphasis on negativity and loss, was important for Kristeva, and helped her with the project of developing notions of horror, *jouissance* and death.

Julia Kristeva's notion of negativity was linked to the relationship between the semiotic and the symbolic as found in the Law of the Father. Kristeva's 'heretical notion' of the 'imaginary father' (E. Grosz, 1992, 199) is the space or position that the father takes up in the mother's desire – he embodies love (*agape* rather than *eros*). In Kristeva's theory, the 'imaginary father' is necessary for the child so that it can grow away from being too dependent on the mother, and then develop a place as a signifying subject.

Georges Bataille's cultivation of the ambivalent aspects of life (such as Sigmund Freud's death-drive and horror) helped Julia Kristeva to formulate her philosophy of loss, negativity and the abject. Kristeva speaks often of 'drives', which're not behind all human behaviour, rather they are 'already semiotic' energy charges which 'extract the body from its homogeous expanse and turn it into a space bound to exterior space; they are the forces which trace the *chora* of the process' (*Polylogue*, 69).

Similarly, Julia Kristeva often uses words such as 'process' and 'practice': her theory always has its practical, physical component: it is not abstracted into nothing but theory. The 'key moment in practice' is transgression. The link between practice and process is defined by Kristeva in *Revolution in Poetic Language*:

> Practice is determined by the pulverization of the unity of consciousness by a nonsymbolized outside, on the basis of objective contradictions and, as such, it is the place where the signifying *process* is carried out. (R, 203)

The political concerns of Marxism and Maoism came to the fore when Julia Kristeva went to China in 1974 with Roland Barthes, Philippe Sollers, François Wahl and Marcelin Pleynet: *Des Chinoises* (*About Chinese Women*), the first of Kristeva's books to be published in English, was the result of this trip. It was 1974's *La Révolution de la langage poétique*, though, that really made Kristeva's name as a philosopher and critic (when she was 33). This was the book that introduced Kristeva's influential notion of the *chora* and the semiotic realm. Kristeva explored the concept of 'poetic language', as distinct from 'ordinary' language, in the writers that became staple Kristevan material in subsequent books (such as Antonin Artaud, Marquis de Sade, Comte de Lautréamont, Stéphane Mallarmé, James Joyce, Jean Racine, William Shakespeare, Ferdinand Céline and Louis Wolfson). In approaching her theory of semiotics, Kristeva worked through Edmund Husserl's phenomenology, Louis Hjelmslvian glose-matics, Lacanian psychoanalysis and the referrentiality of Gottlob Frege (M. Payne, 176).

In 1979 Julia Kristeva became a practising psychoanalyst – while keeping the chair in linguistics at the University of Paris VII. The concerns of psychoanalysis, poetic language, gender, maternity and identity were preferred Kristevan topics during the 1970s and 1980s. She wrote lucidly on painting – in "Giotto's Joy" and "Motherhood According to Bellini", among others (the essays were collected in *Polylogue*); on American society (in "D'Ithaca à New York" and "Why the United States?" among other essays); on the psychoanalysis of abjection (*Pouvoir de l'horreur*) and depression (*Soleil noir*); on racism in France (*Etrangers à nous-mêmes*); and on the history of love poetry and narratives (*Histoire d'amour*). Kristeva has also written fictions, such as *Les Samouraïs* and *The Old and the Wolves,* which represent a movement into the more lyrical territory of Hélène Cixous and Luce Irigaray.

Life as an exile from Bulgaria and a 'foreigner' in France may have further influenced Julia Kristeva's notion of the 'outsider'. For her, the two things, exile and the feminine, became intertwined. Kristeva has stated that her interest in psychoanalysis arose partly from being exiled from Bulgaria (*Partisan Review*, 1986, 216). Being an exile helped Kristeva see both her own country and her adopted country more clearly.[3] Her experience of displacement was an ingredient in her idea of the 'cosmo-politan' individual, the 'intellectual dissident'. As Kristeva knows, strangeness or otherness (being a foreigner) is fundamental to being human: as Kristeva put it, *étrangers à nous-mêmes* (we are strangers to our-selves). In *Strangers to Ourselves* Kristeva describes the foreigner as the 'cold orphan', motherless, a 'devotee of solitude', a 'fanatic of absence', alone even in a crowd, arrogant, rejected, yet oddly happy (SO, 4-5). The stranger is always in motion, doesn't belong anywhere, to 'any time, any love' (SO, 7).

Julia Kristeva was critical of the politicization of sexual 'difference', which she saw in the work of Hélène Cixous, Luce Irigaray, and the Psych et Po group; 'it is all too easy to pass from the search for *difference* to the denigration of the symbolic', Kristeva wrote in a 1979 article, "Il n'y a pas de maître à langage" (134-5). Kristeva describes the essentialist (second wave) view of feminism as 'the second stage' of feminism, post-1968, and part of 'female time' (S. Lefanu, 175). The first stage of feminism had been suffragism and Existential feminism, the struggle for equality, up to the 1960s (and identified with 'male time'). For Kristeva, the struggle against phallogocentrism and the monologic of patriarchy, might 'sink into an essentialist cult of *Woman*' (ib.). However, in *Women's Time*, Kristeva acknowledges that the new, post-second wave feminism will

> henceforth be situated on the terrain of the inseparable conjunction of the sexual and the symbolic, in order to try to discover, first, the specificity of the female, and then, in the end, that of each individual woman. (K, 196)

Julia Kristeva spoke of 'demassifications' of power, which can only occur because the first phase of feminism had asserted equal rights for women. Kristeva is sceptical of second wave feminism, and of the insistence on (lesbian) separatism. For Kristeva, language is a pre-condition of social life, so the Law of the Father seems inevitable; Kristeva does not believe a society could be matriarchal except in name only.

Critics and feminists have been disappointed by Julia Kristeva's apparent avoidance of the traditional or political roles of feminism (in statements such as

> while a certain feminism takes its pouting and its violation for protest and perhaps even for dissidence, genuine feminine innovation... will not be possible until we have elucidated motherhood, feminine creation, and the relationship between them. (1977, 6)

Julia Kristeva says she is committed to feminism, but her attitude towards the women's or feminist movement is ambivalent. For example, Kristeva regards the notion in feminism of 'for-women-only' with suspicion, for it relies on 'a kind of mythicizing of femininity', a reliance on a pseudo-Existential concept of woman, a view of 'woman' which 'attaches a guilt complex to the maternal function', so that having children renders the woman 'not good for anything' (interview, 1977, 106/8). For Simone de Beauvoir, 'women will not be liberated until they are liberated from children, and children are at the same time to some degree liberated from adults' (in M, 146).

For Elizabeth Grosz, a major failing of Julia Kristeva's philosophy is her lack of consideration of the relation between bodies (sexuality) and expression. For Grosz, corporeality is 'always sexually specific and concrete', but Kristeva doesn't acknwoledge this, or doesn't provide any answers:

> In her understanding, there can be no specific female writing, no female text, but only texts about women or evoking a lost, renounced femininity and maternity, as do (patriarchal forms of) religious discourse and poetical texctual transgressions. This, it seems to be, is a major problem for Kristeva's work. (1990, 101)

For Elizabeth Grosz, the body isn't simply a natural or organic thing or process; there is always a lot more going on with the body – to do with the cultural, social and psychological impact on it, as she explains in her stunning book *Volatile Bodies*:

> What psychoanalytic theory makes clear is that the body is literally written on, inscribed, by desire and signification, at the anatomical, physiological, and neurological levels. The body is in sense naturally or innately psychical, sexual, or sexed. It is indeterminate and indeter-minable outside its social constitution as a body of a particular type. This implies that the body which it presumes and helps to explain is an open-ended, pliable set of significations, capable of being rewritten, reconstituted, in quite other terms than those which mark it, and consequently capable of reinscribing the forms of sexed identity and psychical subjectivity at work today. (60-61)

As Elizabeth Grosz reminds us, human beings always live in their bodies: they always have a body. They can't remain human without a body:

> Human subjects never simply *have* a body; rather, the body is always necessarily the object and subject of attitudes and judgements. It is psychically invested, never a matter of indifference. Human being love their bodies (or, what amounts libidinally to the same thing, they hate them or parts of them). The body never has merely instrumental or

utilitarian value for the subject. (ib., 81)

Even when it is nude, the body exhibits traces of its culture, its society, its politics, its use, and its practices, as Grosz notes:

> The naked European/ American/ African/ Asian/ Australian body (and clearly even within these categories there is enormous cultural variation) is still marked by its disciplinary history, by its habitual patterns of movement, by the corporeal commitments it has undertaken in day-to-day life. It is in no sense a natural body, for it is as culturally, racially, sexually, possibly even as class distinctive, as it would be it if were clothed.

In the advanced capitalist, technological world, the body is not a 'natural' form any more, as Elizabeth Grosz explains in *Volatile Bodies*: clothing, exercise, jewellery, lifestyle, habits, negotiations of the cultural and social as well as the physical environment, and all sorts of activities alter it, inscribe it, turn it into something definitely not 'natural':

> Makeup, stilettos, bras, hair sprays, clothing, underclothing mark women's bodies, whether black or white, in ways in which hair styles, professional training, personal grooming, gait, posture, body building, and sports may mark men's. There is nothing natural or ahistorical about these modes of corporeal inscriptions. Through then, bodies are make amenable to the prevailing exigencies of power. They make the flesh into a particular type of body – pagan, primitive, medieval, capitalist, Italian, American, Australian. (142)

Jennifer Stone asserts that 'Kristeva's work is no longer in women's interests' (1983, 42), while Mary Russo calls her 'post-feminist' (in F. Barker). Kristeva is seen as reinforcing traditional notions of 'femininity', encouraging the binary configurations of biologism and sexual difference. The Marxist-Feminist Literature Collective called Kristeva's poetics 'politically unsatisfactory',[4] while for Allon White, Kristeva is politically ineffective (16). In "Oscillation du 'pouvoir' au 'refus'" (1974), Kristeva speaks of the negative function women may hold, its potential to explode social codes, its revolutionary moments (in M, 166).

Elizabeth Grosz has criticized Julia Kristeva's notions of gender and the semiotic/ symbolic modalities: her 'ideal model of a transgressive subjectivity articulating itself is a male who has identified with and taken upon himself representation of a femininity women can't speak: man mimicking the woman who reproduce the man!' (in C. Pateman, 131). Gayatri Chakravorty Spivak is also critical of Kristeva's poetics, the way in which Kristeva equates the literary *avant garde* with political radic-alism (in "French feminism in an international frame"). Critics have spoken of the disappointing performance of French feminist theory when it is put into practice. The *écriture féminine* of Cixous and Kristeva seemed, at first, to subvert masculine realism, but the largely masculine literary canon remained in place. As one critic said, '[i]t has proved easier to look for the semiotic chora in *Ulysses* than in, say, suffragette autobiographies of the period' (J. Radford, 1989, 96).

Other critics have been disappointed by continental feminism as a whole: for all its radical analysis of phallologocentrism, colonialism, and the harmful aspects of Western civilization, it then retreats from following through the implications of its analysis. It goes so far then stops. 'Continental feminism would seem to be the most potentially radical current in contemporary political theory', wrote Laura Kipnis in 1989 (209), but it was also prone to deliberately distancing itself from political praxis, to æstheticization, and to theoretical autonomy. Even as French and European feminism identifies a new political subject, it 'is then paralyzed by this knowledge and by its own First World status, hysterically blind to the geopolitical implications of its own program' (ib., 209). French feminism appears to be prevented from acting politically or advocating certain political practices by its own hyper-sensitivity, its acute self-consciousness. Perhaps, Kipnis suggests, the worlds of economic and political power do not have much to do with *jouissance*, the semiotic realm, the pre-œdipal, sexual fluids and mediæval female mystics. Maybe, but Cixous, Irigaray and Kristeva have continued to engage with political and social issues throughout their careers; they have never shied away from them.

✤

Hélène Cixous, Luce Irigaray and Julia Kristeva all have different modes of writing. There are times when they are writing in the sober, measured tones of a cultural critic, philosopher or psychoanalyst. They have strident feminist voices (Cixous and Irigaray more than Kristeva). They have personal reminiscence modes. They have a relaxed, informal mode in interviews. And, most powerful of all, they have lyrical modes. Thus, Cixous, the most 'poetic' of the three, will break into a visionary, ultra-lyrical way of writing. With books such as *Powers of Horror*, Kristeva's work became more personal. In "Stabat Mater", Kristeva wrote passionately of her experience of childbirth:

> Nights of wakefulness, scattered sleep, sweetness of the child, warm mercury in my arms, cajolery, affection, defenceless body, his or mine, sheltered, protected. A wave swells again, when he goes to sleep, under my skin – tummy, thighs, legs: sleep of the muscles, not of the brain, sleep of the flesh. The wakeful tongue quietly remembers another withdrawal, mine: a blossoming heaviness in the middle of the bed, of a hollow, of the sea... (K, 171-2)

Luce Irigaray, too, changes – though less frequently than Hélène Cixous – from a critical to a lyrical form. Thus, in a piece such as "When Our Lips Speak Together", Irigaray will write poetic sentences such as '[k]iss me. Two lips kiss two lips, and openness is ours again.' This is the kind of phrase which never appears in most cultural theorists outside of quotation marks. One doesn't find Jacques Derrida, Jacques Lacan, Gilles Deleuze, Jean Baudrillard, Jean François Lyotard, Mikhail Bakhtin, Michel Foucault, Louis Althusser, Fredric Jameson, Roland Barthes or Jean-Paul Sartre writing 'kiss me' very often. Well, perhaps Foucault and Barthes said 'kiss me' in darkened hotel rooms – but not in scholarly books published by Minuit or Gallimard.

What marks Hélène Cixous, Luce Irigaray and Julia Kristeva apart from many cultural theorists and philosophers, then, is this personal, confessional and poetic way of writing, where they directly address the reader as the other, the 'you' in an intimate relationship. Derrida,

Foucault, Baudrillard, de Certeau, Eagleton and Jakobson are rarely, if ever, this personal. Cixous, Irigaray and Kristeva, then, are more than simply cultural critics, shuffling between the café and the university library, lighting their pipes (Freud) or chainsmoking cigarettes (Sartre), or bitching about America (any French intellectual), while they ponder on imponderables, chat about prostitutes and brothels with their cronies and write up the occasional philosophical paper.

Hélène Cixous, Luce Irigaray and Julia Kristeva are considerable poets as well as psychoanalysts and philosophers. Their writings have a tremendous *verve*, even when they are dealing with the arid heights of abstruse semiological theory. Kristeva, for example, in writing of childbirth in "Stabat Mater", foregrounds her own experience in ways which many masculinist cultural critics do not, would not, or could not. Kristeva very deliberately places her own experience of something very much in the province of 'women's experience' in a cultural theory essay. Of course, masculinist critics and writers have oft discussed sex, violence and death from 'first hand' experience, so to speak (Marquis de Sade, Georges Bataille, Jean-Paul Sartre and Michel Foucault), but for Kristeva the experience of motherhood decentres men and masculinist theory (C. Burke, 1980).

Feminist theorists and poets such as Hélène Cixous, Luce Irigaray and Julia Kristeva are valuable, then, precisely because they foreground experiences that have been sidelined or stereotyped for centuries. Kristeva's account of childbirth knocks away conventional accounts, such as from traditional science and medicine, or from the early Christian 'fathers', such as St Augustine, who maintained, in the bizarre way of his, that people are born between fæces and urine. The French feminists counter this demonization of female sexuality and make it a central part of their study. The effect of such foregrounding of female sexuality is disruptive and subversive. As Luce Irigaray said in *This Sex Which Is Not One*: 'what is most strictly forbidden to women today is that they should attempt to express their own pleasure' (I, 125).

Experience itself is not to be sidelined, as Elizabeth Grosz has suggested in *Volatile Bodies*, but is a useful issue in feminism: Grosz has drawn on the philosophy of Maurice Merleau-Ponty in this regard. However, experience is also culturally conditioned:

> Experience is not outside social, political, historical, and cultural forces and in this sense cannot provide an outside vantage point from which to judge them. Merleau-Ponty's understanding of the constructed, synthetic nature of experience, its simultaneously active and passive functioning, its role in both the inscription and subversion of socio-political values, provides a crucial confirmation of many feminists' unspoken assumptions regarding women's experiences. (94-95)

Hélène Cixous, Luce Irigaray and Julia Kristeva pull language apart and remake it. They often put words in parentheses and quotes, or split them up, or hyphenate them. Word plays such as 'specula(riza)tion' are common in their work. They parody classic texts and draw attention to hypocrisy and banality. They snuggle up close to classic philosophic texts and parody them in order to bring out the blind spots, repressions and hypocrisies. Irigaray uses mimicry and pastiche to interrogate philosophy; she has rewritten Friedrich Nietzsche and Sigmund Freud, much as Monique Wittig has reworked Dante Alighieri and Miguel Cervantes, and Cixous has tackled Greek mythology, Freud and the *Bible*.

In particular, words such as *il* and *elle,* the gendering of French words, is central to their reworking of language and philosophy. This makes their writing particularly difficult to translate, because they are moving back and forth, continually, between received and ironic/ polemical treatments of language. Thus, translators and editors are forced to interject, and set words in square brackets [like this], in order to remind the reader of the original French text. Hélène Cixous and Luce Irigaray are the most playful in this respect: for this reason, their texts should always, ideally, be quoted in the French and in translation. However, as this is a study written in English, I have not assumed that readers can read French, so I have generally drawn on the English translations of Cixous, Irigaray and Kristeva that are available. Where possible, I have used the collections of writings or *Readers* of Cixous, Irigaray and Kristeva (*The Hélène Cixous*

Reader (Routledge), *The Irigaray Reader* (Blackwell) and *The Kristeva Reader* (Blackwell)), as these are generally available. These are scholarly, well-edited selections of key works of Cixous, Irigaray and Kristeva. Unfortunately, many of the English translations of Cixous, Irigaray and Kristeva are published in less widely available editions (by University of Minnesota Press, Columbia University Press, Harvard University Press, Athlone Press and Cornell University Press). These are excellent editions, but Cixous, Irigaray and Kristeva have not been taken up by a mainstream publisher – their works remain available only in large or specialist or online stores. (Kristeva's official website is: kristeva.fr).

French writers are especially prone to word games (and critics sometimes try to ape them, desperate to show off). The trouble with word games and puns is that they often come across as immature, ponpous, and kinda pointless. Showy, self-conscious. 'Look at me! Look what I can do with L-Ah-nN^^Nn<>Goo-u[1234567890]-A-g-e.'

2

FRENCH FEMINIST POETICS: THE ISSUES OF FEMINIST AND WOMEN'S ART

One of the problems that feminists have addressed with regard to women's art is: can there be a truly 'female' or 'feminine' or 'women's' art? Is art made by women (women's art) ever completely free of patriarchal influences, structures, forms? Can there be a women's art that exists in its own female space, away from patriarchy and masculinist ideas and experiences? Julia Kristeva is pessimistic on this contentious issue. For her, there has been no 'female writing' thus far in our culture. She said in 1977:

> If we confine ourselves to the *radical* nature of what is today called 'writing', that is, if we submit meaning and the speaking subject in

language to a radical examination and then reconstitute them in a more polyvalent than fragile manner, there is nothing in either past or recent publications by women that permits us to claim that a specifically female writing exists.[1]

In French feminism the text is primary, and a text can be 'feminine' regardless of who creates it. For Hélène Cixous a man can write a 'feminine' text (such as Jean Genet). In "Sorties", where Cixous provides a list of oppositions, the ones on the 'night' or 'feminine' side are the ones most often associated with poetry: 'mother', 'heart', 'sensitive', 'moon', 'night', 'nature' (M, 90). For Cixous, most writing, by men or women, is masculine. She writes:

> Most women are like this; they do someone else's – man's – writing, and in their innocence sustain it and give it voice, and end up producing writing that's in effect masculine.[2]

The notion of '*écriture féminine*' of Luce Irigaray and Hélène Cixous, which's much discussed in feminist literary criticism,[3] is rejected by Monique Wittig. Wittig also rejects the notion of 'man' and 'woman'. For her, 'woman' is a historical, political, ideological and cultural construct. She writes that "woman' has meaning only in heterosexual systems of thought and heterosexual economic systems'.[4]

The discussion of women's art and women artists is, many feminists feel, crucial to feminism. After all, *one knows what male artists are like*, and we are utterly familiar with male art. People are surrounded, embedded, drenched, choked, smothered by patriarchal art and culture, by male-orientated – even if not specifically male-*made* – culture. Male projections, often onto women, have become dogma. Masculinist fears of the body, and sexuality, have been projected onto women, so that the vagina becomes a hell hole, the 'gateway to Hell'. As Luce Irigaray writes: men's '*fantasies lay down the law*'.[5] In a patriarchal culture, male art is seen as the hegemony which (female) feminists have to subvert. For too long, some feminists claim, women's art has been defined as simply 'not male'/ 'men's art'. It is defined by its non-inclusion in the traditional sphere of men's/ male/ masculine art. As Irigaray puts it in *Je, tu, nous*: '[b]eing a woman is equated with not being a man' (Je, 71).

There are many feminists who advocate the exaltation of all manner of women artists, who argue for a women's art based on women artists, who want people to look at women artists. There are other feminists who deny the primacy of the author, who say that the work – the text – is primary, who deny the transparency of the text (this is one of Julia Kristeva's projects).

Toril Moi and many other feminist critics have questioned the humanist notion of 'realism' or 'authenticity', where a text is seen to reflect the actual experience of the one who created it. Humanist criticism sees a direct relation between author and text, assuming that the artwork is a direct expression of the artist's experience. Artists, however, know that very often the artwork ends up being far away from what they intended to express or communicate. Mary Ellan sees the Western world as dominated by sexualization; she calls it 'thought by sexual analogy', which urges nearly all experience to be classified 'by means of sexual analogy'.[7]

Hélène Cixous says, in the famous article "The Laugh of the Medusa", '[a]nd why don't you write? Write! Writing is for you, you are for you... Write, let no one hold you back, let nothing stop you' (M, 246-7). For Cixous (who is loved and loathed by feminists nearly as energetically as Andrea Dworkin or Germaine Greer or Princess Diana), writing is absolutely crucial, and central; it is oxygen to her, she must write to live, as she says:

> Having never been without writing, having writing in my body, at my throat, on my lips... to me my texts are elements of a whole which interweaves my own story. ("Preface", C, xv)

One can 'read' creatively, if one doesn't write. Much of feminist theory is based on 'reading' texts as a woman, a feminist, a lesbian. If the author is 'dead', and the text is primary, then deeply engaging with texts is crucial. Hence the importance, too, of feminist æsthetic and philosophic criticism, which aims to interpret all manner of texts. The reader, at least, is 'real'. The reader, it would seem, is truly flesh and blood, not a linguistic abstraction. Even here, though, some feminists dispute the 'reality' or 'authenticity' of the body, for the body, like education or desire or the family, is culturally and socially conditioned. That is, there is no such thing as a 'pure' reality, a 'pure' experience, a 'pure' response to a text, a response that is not modulated by all manner of social, societal, familial, psychological, political, ideological and cultural influences. In feminism, the scenario is not simply a woman and a book, existing completely separately from everything else, in some utopian place. No, there is so much that gets in the way of the seemingly 'innocent' or 'pure' exchange between a woman and an artwork, a person and a text. But the personal response is crucial, and alive. Reading can be, in itself, radical and transformative.

JULIA KRISTEVA'S POETICS

Creating a 'feminist æsthetics' means writing/ rewriting language, art, culture, notions of knowledge and ontology, of identity and politics, all manner of things. For Julia Kristeva, there is no 'other place' in language, for, as Ludwig Wittgenstein said, the world humans live in is a world circumscribed by language. In effect, language 'writes' the world: to go beyond it is the quest for the 'wild zone', the utterly Other Place. For Kristeva, revolution must occur *within* symbolic (that is, patriarchal) language.[8]

> Literature appears to me as the privileged place where meaning is elaborated and destroyed, where it slips away when one might think that it is being renewed. (J. Kristeva, TL, 279)

Women's writing or art becomes a literature of absence, of negative capability, revealing by what it does not reveal, forever outside yet also inside patriarchal discourse. As the Marxist-Feminist Literature Collective write:

> Women, who are speaking subjects but partially excluded from culture, find modes of expression which the hegemonic discourse cannot integrate. Whereas the eruptive word cannot make the culturally inaccessible, it can surely speak its absence.[8]

Julia Kristeva is much more uncertain about the notion of 'women's writing' than Hélène Cixous or Luce Irigaray. Kristeva often frames her feelings on the subject with a series of questions expressing doubts. It is worth remembering that despite her uncertainty, Kristeva has studied artists (in particular writers) in much greater detail than Cixous or Irigaray. She asks questions which are central to feminist æsthetics and women's art. Will there be a visionary feminism which takes women's art (French feminists use the term 'writing' to cover cultural/ creative activities) into a new era?

> Or is it [asks Kristeva], on the contrary and as avant-garde feminists hope, that having started with the idea of difference, feminism will be able to break free of its belief in woman, her power, her writing, so as to channel this demand for difference into each and every element of the female whole, and, finally, to bring out the singularity of each woman, and beyond this, her multiplicities, her plural languages, beyond the horizon, beyond sight, beyond faith itself? (*Women's Time*, K, 208)

Julia Kristeva is very positive, though, despite her insistence on absence. She is uncompromizing; in "Freud and Love", she says she believes in the 'notion of emptiness, which is at the heart of the human psyche' (TL, 23). Yet she is optimistic, too. Her philosophy is founded on absence, but she often writes of the possibility that an otherness has been neglected, that there maybe a nighttime space, of the unconscious, of magic or otherness.[10] In *Women's Time* she asks more questions:

Is it because, faced with social norms, literature reveals a certain knowledge and sometimes the truth itself about an otherwise repressed nocturnal, secret and unconscious universe? Because it thus redoubles the social contract by exposing the unsaid, the uncanny? (K, 207)

And, again from *Women's Time*, Julia Kristeva argues for aspects of female subjectivity that could exist outside of patriarchy:

As for time, female subjectivity would seem to provide a specific measure that essentially retains *repetition* and *eternity* from among the multiple modalities of time known through the history of civilizations. On the one hand, there are cycles, gestation, the eternal recurrence of a biological rhythm which conforms to that of nature and imposes a temporality whose stereotypes shock, but whose regularity and unison with what is experienced as extra-subjective time, cosmic time, occasion vertiginous visions and unnameable *jouissance*. On the other hand, and perhaps as a consequence, there is the massive presence of a monumental temporality, without cleavage or escape, which has so little to do with linear time (which passes) that the very word 'temporality' hardly fits: all-encompassing and infinite like imaginary space, this temporality reminds one of Kronos in Hesiod's mythology, the incestuous son whose massive presence covered all of Gaea in order to separate her from Ouranos, the father. (*Women's Time*, in K, 191)

Questioned about the possibility of an *écriture féminine*, Julia Kristeva replied that she was 'very uncertain on this point'. Kristeva vouches for a plurality of subjectivities and positions, a plurality of ways of writing. However, she acknowledges that most, or all, artists have to relate to the archaic mother and the semiotic modality at some time or other. This is her common denominator among creative people, this relationship with the archaic mother. But this identification with the mother involves more risks for the female writer than for the male writer. The fear is that 'I might lose myself, lose my identity' (QS, 132). There seems to be more at stake for the woman artist in Kristeva's view. Using the metaphor of the Orphic descent into Hell or underworld, which is one of the primary analogies of the creative quest, Kristeva says:

This explains why perhaps it's more difficult for women to get out of hell, this descent: Orpheus manages it but Eurydice doesn't. (ib.)

FRENCH FEMINISM AND FRIEDRICH NIETZSCHE

Friedrich Nietzsche (1844-1900) has been one of the major philosophic encounters in the work of Luce Irigaray, and to a lesser extent in the work of Hélène Cixous and Julia Kristeva. Recent feminist analyses of Nietzsche's philosophy have gone far beyond the stereotype of Nietzsche as a misogynist: his relation to the 'feminine', with 'woman' and 'women', is much more complicated than mere woman-hating and sexism.[9]

Every intellectual and writer seems to have to grapple with Friedrich Nietzsche at some time or other (especially the French philosophers: Georges Bataille, Cixous, Sarah Kofman, Gilles Deleuze, Jacques Derrida and Jean-Paul Sartre). For Derrida, Nietzsche's relationship with the feminine was embodied by his identification with three types of women: the castrating woman, the castrated woman, and the affirming woman. 'Nietzsche was all these', wrote Derrida – sometimes at once, successively or simultaneously.[11] For some feminist critics, the figure behind these masks may be Nietzsche's mother, and his ambiguous relationship with his mother may inform some of his ambivalent attitudes towards women.[12]

The influence of Lou Andreas-Salomé (1861-1937) on Friedrich Nietzsche has been noted by some feminist critics, including French feminist Sarah Kofman. Nietzsche was besotted with Andreas-Salomé, calling her 'sharp-sighted as an eagle and courageous as a lion'.[13] Andreas-Salomé was the only erotic/ philosophic focus in Nietzsche's otherwise celibate experience of women.[13] Kofman has wondered whether Andreas-Salomé was a model for that narcissistic woman which men love, the type that demands to be loved. Kofman considers this narcissistic woman in relation to Nietzsche, and wonders whether Andreas-Salomé was the mediator of the theory of narcissism between Nietzsche and Sigmund Freud.[14] Andreas-Salomé's notion of the narcissistic woman, and her thoughts on the artist, influenced Nietzsche.

In the Nietzschean-Andreas-Saloméan view, the (male) artist, if he is lucky, can aspire to the creativity of the woman, to become a 'birther' (*Gebärerin*), which may make him 'more whole, more organic, fused... with what he creates, just as woman is,' Andreas-Salomé wrote in her 1899 essay "Die in such ruhende Frau": 'and maintains him as it were in a joy of spiritual pregnancy, which lives deep within itself.'[15] Luce Irigaray was sceptical of such a project. Other critics have analyzed Hélène Cixous' reading of Nietzsche.[16]

Julia Kristeva's relation to Friedrich Nietzsche has been less important than in Hélène Cixous and Luce Irigaray. Jacques Lacan and Sigmund Freud figure much larger in Kristeva's theory than Nietzsche. Kristeva is sceptical of Nietzsche's philosophy in *About Chinese Women*, when she writes: 'Nietzsche would not have known how to be a woman. A woman has nothing to laugh about when the symbolic order collapses' (K, 150). Even so, some critics have seen similarities between the philosophies of Kristeva and Nietzsche, between the notion of rebirth (in Kristeva's interpretation of melancholy and Nietzsche's revaluation of values).[17] Nietzsche's relation to the maternal is more in tune with Kristeva's poetics. Nietzsche's problem was that he conflated 'woman', the 'feminine' and motherhood: in his works, woman becomes 'the fetish of eternal pregnancy', a phallic mother of eternal potency: sexually, she is feared, but as a mother she is exalted.[18] For Sigmund Freud, the fetish was a substitute for the missing penis of the mother, a view that perpetuated the fantasy of the phallic mother; Nietzsche fetishized the womb and women's (spiritual) fecundity. He spoke in Goddess-oriented terms, the kind familiar from thousands of years of mythology and poetry, of the 'eternally creative primordial mother'.[19] In "Fetishization", Elizabeth Grosz is illuminatingly clear:

The fetishist demands, in spite of recognizing its impossibility, that there be a maternal phallus. He simultaneously affirms and denies that the mother is castrated... Fetishization renders the object into an image of another, genital object, thereby sexualizing it and making it into an appropriate or worthy object of desire for the subject. It thus describes a common male mode of objectification of women's bodies. (1992, 117)

JACQUES LACAN AND FRENCH FEMINISM

For French feminists such as Hélène Cixous, Jacques Lacan's (1901-81) philosophy of the Lacanian 'lack' is ridiculous. As she writes in "The Laugh of the Medusa": '[w]hat's a desire originating from a lack? A pretty meagre desire' (M, 262). And Luce Irigaray and other feminists (Sarah Kofman, Elizabeth Grosz, Michèle Montrelay and Mary Ann Doane) have criticized the Freudian-Lacanian emphasis on the phallus as the 'transcendental signifier', as the measure of authentic sexual pleasure.[20] What woman lacks is lack itself, says Montrelay, an inability to create distance and representation.

From Plato to Sigmund Freud and Jacques Lacan the desire and lack has been central to Western sexual metaphysics: in this negative model, one is doomed to a desire for more and more consumption, which leads to dissatisfaction. Freudian-Lacanian desire can never be satisfied: dissatisfaction is built-in. Desire is never annihilated: for Georg Wilhelm Hegel, only another desire can satisfy desire and also perpetuate it. Desire thus desires more desire (this has a vivid expression in late capitalist consumerism, where it is always the *next* commodity that will truly satisfy and stop the hunger for more objects. But it never happens).

Far better to see desire, as Elizabeth Grosz does, as a positive force, one which (following Benedictus de Spinoza and Friedrich Nietzsche as opposed to Hegel and Freud), makes connections and alliances. Instead of regarding desire as a repetitive search for something to make up for a central, gaping loss, it is seen as a force of production and creative assemblage; not fantasmatic but real.[21]

This view of desire (in the work of Friedrich Nietzsche, Spinoza, Gilles Deleuze and Félix Guattari) is also that of Hélène Cixous and Luce Irigaray (Julia Kristeva seems to be less convinced, and more committed to a post-Lacanian reading of desire). Desire becomes not yearning but actualization, actions, creation: instead of a Lacanian lack, desire becomes primary. As Cixous says: 'my desires have invented new desires' (M, 246).

The poetic moment, for Julia Kristeva, is founded on desire: desire is what keeps the system together:

> The other that will guide you and itself through this dissolution is a rhythm, music, and within language, a text. But what is the connection that holds you both together? Counter-desire, the negative of desire, inside-out desire, capable of questioning (or provoking) its own infinite quest. Romantic, filial, adolescent, exclusive, blind and Oedipal: it is all that, but for others. It returns to where you are, both of you, disappointed, irritated, ambitious, in love with history, critical, on the edge and even in the midst of its own identity crisis. (DL, 165)

On desire, Julia Kristeva writes, in "Psychoanalysis and the Polis":

> Desire, the discourse of desire, moves towards its object through a connection, by displacement and deformation. The discourse of desire becomes a discourse of delirium when it forecloses its object, which is always already marked by that 'minus factor' mentioned earlier, and when it establishes itself as the complete locus of *jouissance* (full and without exteriority). In other words, no other exists, no object survives in its irreducible alterity. (K, 308)

The Lacanian Look emphasizes eroticism. Seeing is erotic, the eye becomes a kind of phallus, caressing the obscure object of desire, which it can never 'possess'. As the poet Rainer Maria Rilke wrote: '[g]azing is a wonderful thing.'[23] The act of looking eroticizes the object. Jack Zipes explains in *Don't Bet On the Prince*:

For [Lacan], seeing is desire, and the eye functions as a kind of phallus. However, the eye cannot clearly see its object of desire, and in the case of male desire, the female object of desire is an illusion created by the male unconscious. Or, in other words, the male desire for woman expressed in the gaze is auto-erotic and involves the male's desire to have his own identity reconfirmed in a mirror image. (1986, 258)

The Look is an assertion of male power and sexuality. For the gaze is male, or masculine, and feminists have grappled with the notion of a 'female' gaze.[24] 'Male desire is presented as a response to female beauty', writes Andrea Dworkin in *Intercourse* (114). Margaret Whitford glosses Luce Irigaray's work in 1991 thus:

Western systems of representation privilege *seeing*: what can be seen (presence) is privileged over what cannot be seen (absence) and guarantees Being, hence the privilege of the penis which is elevated to the status of the Phallus. (30)

Lacanian psychoanalysis is a hell of misrepresentations and misreadings, mirrors and imaginary spaces. The subject in the Lacanian system is constantly trying to make good mistakes made in its early psycho-sexual growth. In the dreaded mirror phase, the image becomes a mirage, and a distance is set up between the image and the body, an absence which Lacan termed the *objet a*. In the confusions of the three realms, the symbolic, real and imaginary, the subject cannot realize what it most wants to realize. The objects of desire remain forever elusive.

There is something inexplicably depressing about Lacan's version of psycho-sexual events. Lovers, in the Lacanian system, desire what they cannot have. The problem of the lack, the *objet a* and *la chose*, can never be resolved. Lacanian philosophy posits, among other things (here we go again): an eternal search for what can never be found.[25] The Freudian-Lacanian system demands a continuous series of substitutions for objects to fill the primordial lack. It is a system of replacing an imaginary and immobile plenitude that will always fail. The primal realm remains always lost or forbidden. The Paradise of early childhood recedes ever further into the distance of the past.

Meanwhile, in the Jungian system, Beatrice, Laura, Cleopatra, Isolde, Eurydice, Ariadne and all those women of myth, poetry and legend, are incarnations of the *anima*, which is, as Carl Jung explains, something all males possess: '[e]very man carries with him the eternal image of woman, not the image of this or that particular woman, but a definitive feminine image.'[26] The *anima* is 'a personification of the unconscious in a man, which appears as a woman or a goddess in dreams, visions and creative fantasies', comment Emma Jung and Marie-Louise von Franz.[27] Male painters throughout history have depicted their version of the *anima*, it seems. Each (male) painter has a version of the 'inner feminine figure' as Jung calls her (1967, 210-1). For painters, this idealized *anima* figure seems to be another manifestation of that obscure object of desire, the eroticized woman, a mirror for male lust. The equation is: the more sublime and voluptuous the woman is painted, the more sublime and voluptuous is the artist's desire. The artist's model, then, can be seen as a Jungian *anima*, heavily eroticized, a Lacanian phallic mirror.

Further: in Lacanian psychology, desire, which is the foundation of the system, is enmeshed with speaking, with creativity and art. The œdipal crisis and the repression of the desire for the mother occurs with the entry into the Symbolic Order, and the entry into language. As Toril Moi crystallizes Jacques Lacan's thought so concisely in *French Feminist Thought*: '[t]o speak as a subject is therefore the same as to represent the existence of repressed desire' (1988, 99-100).

The links between seeing and erotic pleasure, between the eye and the phallus, are found in much of Western 'high culture': not only in the history of painting, but also in the great works of poets such as Dante Alighieri, Francesco Petrarch, William Shakespeare and the troubadours. In the 'classic' text of pornography, Georges Bataille's *The Story of the Eye*, there are eyes placed in mouths, vulvas and anuses. Bataille takes the Sadeian ethic of the pornographic Look to its logical, literal extreme.[28]

Men gaze at women and manipulate them into erotic poses. Larysa Mykyta writes in 1983:

The sexual triumph of the male passes through the eye, through the contemplation of the woman. Seeing the women ensures the satisfaction of wanting to be seen, of having one's desire recognized, and thus comes back to the original aim of the scopic drive. Woman is repressed as subject and desired as object in order to efface the gaze of the Other, the gaze that would destroy the illusion of reciprocity and one-ness that the process of seeing usually supports. The female object does not look, does not have it own point of view; rather it is erected as an image of the phallus sustaining male desire. [29]

The pleasure of the text, whether the text is a painting, film, magazine, photograph, piece of theatre, and so on, comes, according to Roland Barthes, when the Look of the spectator is aligned with that of the author.[30] What feminist criticism has done is to question the masculine 'pleasure of the text', arguing for a feminist reading of the traditional masculine or patriarchal view of texts.

For some feminists, however, there can be no true 'feminist gaze', because the Look is always masculine, ultimately. If the spectator is a 'gendered object', suggests Annette Kuhn in *Women's Pictures*, then 'masculine subjectivity [is] the only subjectivity available' (1982, 63). The politics of representation, which are central to the consumption of culture and art, are weighted firmly in favour of men and patriarchy. As John Berger writes: 'men act and women appear'. And as Catherine King notes:

most images in masculine visual ideology are created to empower men as spectators – that is, to see themselves as endlessly important with things laid out for their desire.[31]

Post-Lacanian feminists such as Luce Irigaray argue that subjectivity can only be attributed to women with difficulty. Irigaray claims that 'any theory of the subject has always been appropriated by the 'masculine'' (S, 133). 'Woman' is tied to a 'non-subjective sub-jectum' (S, 265). Irigaray stresses the sexed being, the sexualized subject and speaking position. No form of knowledge or philosophy can be authentic or 'universal' if it ignores the female position. Irigaray concentrates on the act of enunciation, the act of producing discourse. Irigaray stresses the interiority of

the speaking subject, the traces of subjectivity found in acts of communication. The continual denial of a sexualized discourse threatens the
possibility of an emergent non-patriarchal society. Irigaray has investig-
ated the use by men and women of everyday language, concluding that
men and women privilege different patterns of speech, with men
encouraging their 'self-affection', or relations to/ with the self and the self
projecting in others, while women use language to make connections and
relationships with both sexes. Irigaray's deconstruction of the languages
of science, philosophy and politics has demonstrated the repression of the
feminine – Dale Spender and other feminists have come to similar
conclusions. For Irigaray, this repression is not built into language, but
reflects the (patriarchal) social order. In order to change one the other
must also be changed.

Luce Irigaray says that if the vagina is regarded as a 'hole', it is a
'negative' space that cannot be represented in the dominant discourse:
thus to have a vagina is to be deprived of a voice, to be decentred or
culturally subordinated, and so Irigaray replaces Jacques Lacan's mirror
with a vaginal speculum.[32] The phallic privileging of the masculine 'I'
(penis, phallus, power, identity, soul), means that female sexuality is
rendered 'invisible', just as the vagina is a negative space or void. The
phallus is the divine, beloved mirror, emblem of masculine narcissism.
But the vulva, being a 'black hole', can reflect back nothing. There is no self
there. Male speculations and narcissistic gazes create a male subject: the
mistakes arise when this male subject is equated with the whole world.
The universality of philosophy and psychoanalysis thus becomes founded
on a one-sided (male) view of the world. Male sexuality and narcissism
mistakenly become the basis for the universal model of sexuality in
psychoanalysis. Female sexuality becomes the negative image of male
sexuality, if female subjectivity is considered at all.

Women are supposed to have 'penis envy', a hankering for the
transcendent signifier which will enable them to attain a positive, creative
identity. Freudian 'penis envy' has been rejected by most feminists. One
can see how Luce Irigaray would have upset Jacques Lacan, who founded

his theory of sexuality, like Sigmund Freud, on the primary of the phallus. In the Freudian-Lacanian phallic system, all is unity, identity, singularity (all the way back to that initial 'singularity', the Big Bang). Ambiguity, multiplicity and excess are excluded from this view: Irigaray's project of rewriting Freud and Lacan disrupts the isomorphic unity and replaces it with a series of dense, poetic, parodic discourses, in which female repression is unleashed and the female unconscious is allowed to explode into academic patriarchy. Irigaray's specular project disrupts the insistence in phallic, patriarchal sexuality on one organ (penis), one orgasm or pleasure (male), one identity (male), and one model of representation (masculine). Irigaray's notion of feminine writing disrupts the unitary dimensions of the phallocratic system ('there would be no longer either subject or object', Irigaray wrote of the new 'female syntax' in *This Sex Which Is Not One*, and "oneness' would no longer be privileged' [134]).

3

✺

FRENCH FEMINISM, SEXUALITY,
AND SEXUAL DIFFERENCE

When feminists discuss the body and sexuality, the results are just as controversial as their discussions of issues such as art vs. pornography, or the ways in which female power can be asserted in the social and political arena. Many feminists speak of the sexual superiority of women, or, if not 'superiority', then at least a sexuality that is more sophisticated, more dangerous, more exhilarating, more subtle, and more sensual – well, that amounts to 'superior'. For instance, Xavière Gauthier, a contemporary of Hélène Cixous, Luce Irigaray and Julia Kristeva, says that:

> ...witches [women] are bursting; their entire bodies are desire; their gestures are caresses; their smell, taste, hearing are all sensual. Their pleasure is so violent, so transgressive, so open, so fatal, that men have not yet recovered... Female eroticism is terrifying; it is an earthquake, a

volcanic eruption, a tidal wave. It is disquieting and so is mystified. It is made a mystery.1

This transgressive, terrifying eroticism has not yet really been depicted in art or pornography for feminists. What we get is men's version of it – male ideas of wild eroticism, with violence as a recurring ingredient. Hélène Cixous reckons that women have an 'infinite', 'cosmic' libido, an eroticism which is always in flux, and so minute and subtle, it goes far beyond male/ masculine sexuality.

> Almost everything is yet to be written by women about femininity: about their sexuality, that is, its infinite and mobile complexity, about their eroticization, sudden turn-ons of a certain miniscule-immense area of their bodies; not about destiny, but about the adventure of such and such a drive, about trips, crossings, trudges, abrupt and gradual awakenings, discoveries of a zone at one time timorous and soon to be forthright. A woman's body, with its thousand and one thresholds of ardor... (M, 256)

Women have an all-over, total body eroticism, say writers such as Anaïs Nin, Peter Redgrove and Luce Irigaray (and so do some men!). 'But *woman has sex organs just about everywhere*. She experiences pleasure almost everywhere', writes Luce Irigaray (yes, but so do some men I know!).2 Feminists have spoken of the wildness of women's eroticism and their fantasies. What this stance does is to uphold the eternal philosophical dualism of the West, setting women always against men, and using men to gauge women's sexuality. Feminists such as Hélène Cixous have argued, rightly, that masculine 'binary logic', which constantly opposes terms such as 'masculine' and 'feminine', is very limiting. It is two-term logocentrism, which reduces everything to 'yes' or 'no' (NBW, 63f).

Pornography, like art, pivots around *desire*. And desire, as Hélène Cixous notes, is something that never dies: '[d]esire never dies', she asserts (NBW). Cixous asks in *The Newly Born Woman*:

How do I experience my sexual pleasure?... What is feminine *jouissance*,

where is it sited, how is it inscribed in her body, in her unconscious?
And then, how can it be written? (NBW, 151)

The problem is that *jouissance* operates outside of culture or language:
but, to use *jouissance*, to wield its power, some critics claim, one has to
incorporate it somehow into language and expression. The radical
otherness of *jouissance* becomes distorted and circumscribed if it continues to remain outside of language, or in the body (C. Duchen, 98).

Julia Kristeva writes in *About Chinese Women* that:

> no other civilization seems to have made the principle of sexual differ-
> ence so crystal clear: between the two sexes a cleavage or abyss opens
> up... Monotheistic unity is sustained by a radical separation of the
> sexes: indeed, it is this very separation which is its prerequisite. (K, 141)

✤

One of the most fiercely contended areas of feminism, gay, lesbian, and
queer theory, women's studies, and gender studies (whatever one wants
to call it), is the issue of sexuality, and how it relates to gender, identity,
art, pornography, representation, ideology, and politics. In the realm of
feminism and gender/ gay/ lesbian/ queer sexuality studies, there is no
single narrative thread to follow, but a bewilderingly intricate web of
strands, layers, spaces and realms. The brief discussion that follows of
sexual difference/ sexuality/ identity/ gender issues will not proceed in a
satisfyingly logical and A to B fashion, but in a circular, perhaps spiral,
certainly a squiggly way. In gender/ gay/ lesbian/ queer/ sexuality/
women's studies, what one finds are the commentators, feminists and
writers revolving and rehearsing and gassing about the same issues, time
after time.

Luce Irigaray in her famous description of women's sexuality says
women have an all-over eroticism, a total body sensuality, where the
whole of the skin is alive to touches. 'The whole of my body is sexuate. My
sexuality isn't restricted to my sex and to the sexual act (in the narrow
sense)', writes Irigaray (Je, 53). For some feminists, Irigaray's morphology of female creativity is empowering, 'a challenge to the traditional
construction of feminine morphology where the bodies of women are seen

as receptacles for masculine completeness', wrote Moira Gatens.[3] Other feminists see the emphasis on just one form of female sexuality as a distinctly reductive and inauthentic kind of feminism:

> If we define female subjectivity through universal biological/ libidinal givens [writes Ann Rosalind Jones], what happens to the project of changing the world in feminist directions? Further, is women's sexuality so monolithic that shared, typical femininity does justice to it? What about variations in class, in race, and in culture among women? about changes over time in *one* woman's sexuality? (with men, with women, by herself?) How can one libidinal voice – or the two vulval lips so startlingly presented by Irigaray – speak for all women?[4]

Some feminists (such as Anaïs Nin) argue for multiple sexualities, for a plurality of sexualities, as against the standard, traditional notions of heterosexuality, homosexuality, lesbianism and bisexuality. Some feminists argue for the use of erotic feeling as a political weapon. Instead of denying eroticism, some feminists propound an ethics of glorifying sexuality. The body then becomes the centre, the subject, instead of being merely the object of male lust. Eroticism then becomes a source of power, as Audre Lorde explains:

> The erotic is a resource within each of us that lies in a deeply female and spiritual plane, firmly rooted in the power of our unexpressed or unrecognized feeling.[5]

Women speak of their eroticism in fiction and fantasy as being multi-sensual, not simply a matter of the visual or haptic senses, but of every sense, and more, in a synæsthetic experience.

> In those early mornings it all tasted of sex after a few moments... The whole room seemed full of our commingled, complicated smells. And over and over again I'd come, sometimes still nearly asleep

wrote Sue Miller in *The Good Mother*,[6] while Summer Brenner remarked: 'our bodies made light in a soft room'.[7] Susan Griffin has written powerfully of lesbian eroticism in *Viyella*:

> ...my most profound longings and desires, for intimacy, to know, to touch and be inside the body and soul of another, becoming and separating from, devouring and being devoured, that wild, large, amazing, frightening territory of lovemaking belongs for me not with men, but with women.[8]

Nancy Friday has collected women's fantasies in a number of books: *My Secret Garden, Women On Top* and *Forbidden Flowers.* The fantasies involve lesbianism, group sex, sex with animals, sex with pop and movie stars, rape, anal sex, domination, S/M and all manner of erotic activities. Women's fantasies, like their fictions, are, some feminists believe, wilder, larger, more amazing and more frightening, to use Susan Griffin's words, than male fantasies and fictions. The books of erotic fiction and fantasy by women demonstrate something of the erotic ecstasy of women which, as Xavière Gauthier comments, 'is so violent, so transgressive, so open, so fatal, that men have not yet recovered.'[10]

Luce Irigaray talks about the 'very openness' of women's bodies, 'of their flesh, of their genitals', so that boundaries become difficult to define (I, 112). Irigaray speaks of two kinds of erotic *jouissance* – the phallic kind of orgasm, which men are concerned with and brag about – and the *jouissance* in harmony with a female libidinal economy (I, 45). Irigaray's point is that there are forms of *jouissance* other than the phallocratic model. Incredible though women's sexual fantasies may be, they are always defined in terms of male fantasies, often in terms of difference. Julia Kristeva's form of *jouissance* is not Jacques Lacan's phallic or sexual *jouissance*, but a *jouissance* that is ecstasy. For erotic pleasure, Kristeva uses the term *plaisir* (DL, 160).

LESBIAN, GAY AND QUEER THEORY;
MONIQUE WITTIG AND FRENCH FEMINISM

Some feminists regard sexuality as expressed through performances and gestures, rather than being some essence. Thus heterosexuality itself is not an unchanging institution, but may already be a 'constant parody of itself', as Judith Butler suggests in *Gender Trouble* (1990, 122). Heterosexuality, Butler reckons, is continually imitating itself, always miming its own performances in order to appear 'natural'. Catherine MacKinnon wrote: '[s]exuality is that social process which creates, organizes, expresses, and directs desire, creating the social beings we know as women and men, and their relations create society.'[11] Adrienne Rich, in her influential essay "Compulsory heterosexuality and lesbian existence" (1980), says that heterosexuality is not 'preferred' or chosen, but has to be 'imposed, managed, organized, propagandized, and maintained by force'; for Rich, 'violent structures' are required by patriarchal society in order to 'enforce women's total emotional, erotic loyalty and subservience to men'.

Lesbian, gay and queer cultural theory has continually addressed the problem of identity and gender. There are certain sexual and social 'positions' or 'categories' which are seen as 'outside' the (patriarchal) norms, which may have affinities with the female 'outsider' figures of Julia Kristeva and Luce Irigaray. The lesbian, for instance, is sometimes seen as an 'outsider', like the black woman, or the feminist. Gender and sexual identity categories are becoming increasingly blurred.

For example, there are

- 'physical' lesbians,
- 'natural' lesbians,
- 'cultural' or 'social' lesbians,
- 'male' lesbians (men who position themselves as lesbians).
- men with vaginas and women with penises;
- there are queer butches and aggressive femmes,
- there are F2Ms and lesbians who love men,

- queer queens and drag kings,
- daddy boys and dyke mummies,
- bull daggers,
- porno afro homos,
- transsexual Asians,
- butch bottoms,
- femme tops,
- women and lesbians who fuck men,
- women and lesbians who fuck *like* men,
- lesbians who dress up as men impersonating women,
- lesbians who dress up as straight men in order to pick up gay men,
- butches who dress in fem clothing to feel like a gay man dressing as a woman,
    - femmes butched-out in male drag
    - and butches femmed-out in drag.

Sexual and social identities are continually being blurred, redefined, performed, questioned. Terms such as 'straight' and 'gay', 'hetero' and 'homo'/ 'hommo', are no longer adequate for these multi-layered, postmodern sexual identities. We need multiple genders — millions of genders. Two or three just ain't enough! There are many sexualities – surely as many as there are people, and also more (some people have multiple sexualities).

In lesbian and queer theory there are debates about the penis and the phallus: should lesbian sex involve penetration, which merely mimes heterosexual intercourse and perhaps upholds patriarchal norms? Is the lesbian use of the dildo or strap-on 'subversive' or a parody? Does lesbian S/M mock or emulate straight sex? Is the lesbian butch/ femme social category simplistic and stereotypical? Is lesbian sexuality truly 'outside' patriarchal/ masculinist sexuality?

These are the concerns also of Hélène Cixous, Luce Irigaray and Julia Kristeva – the project of an erotic otherness, of an outside space or wild zone for women, a sexuality undefined and unfettered by masculinist discourse. Cixous especially (in "The Laugh of the Medusa"), has argued for a transgressive, radical, political and passionate form of female sexuality, which will go beyond male sexuality. The project is for a female sexuality that will not be a duplicate of masculinist sexuality, that will go beyond male narcissism, doubling and self-recognition.

Monique Wittig (1935-2003) is another powerful French feminist whose works, like those of Hélène Cixous, Luce Irigaray and Julia Kristeva, have been influential and controversial in the field of feminist cultural debate. Wittig is sometimes grouped with Irigaray and Cixous and the project of *écriture féminine*, but Wittig's view of 'lesbian writing' is not about exalting female difference, for in 'lesbian writing' sex is eliminated as a category. Wittig's works (*Les Guerillères, L'Opoponax, The Lesbian Body,* "The Straight Mind", "One Is Not Born a Woman", and *Virigile, non, Brouillon pour un dictionaire des amantes*) seem to offer a radical view of lesbians. Wittig positions lesbians somewhat as Kristeva and Cixous position women: as societal outsiders. In "The Straight Mind", Wittig sees lesbians as becoming nomads and runaways, as well as becoming more establishment. For Wittig, lesbians are outsiders in the hetero-patriarchal system: Wittig's oft-quoted statement runs thus:

> Lesbian is the only concept I know of which is beyond the categories of sex (woman and man), because the designated subject (lesbian) is *not* a woman, either economically, or politically, or ideologically. (1980, 53)

In *Le corps lesbien*, Monique Wittig transformed the (male/ masculinist) 'I' of Western love poetry into the split 'J/e', the aim being to 'lesbianize the symbols' (1985, 11), so that Orphea saves her Euridice, and Christ becomes 'Christa the much-crucified'. For some feminists, Wittig has created in 'J/e' 'the most powerful lesbian in literature' (Elaine Marks);[13] Wittig's lesbian writings have created a new 'lesbian narrative space',[14] with an 'epistemological shift' away from phallocentrism.[14] Wittig's lesbian writing has nullified the masculinist social position (D. Crowder, 127).

For other feminists, Monique Wittig's project is simply too utopian and impractical: it makes the leap from imagination to representation without considering the practical difficulties of the proto-separatist lesbian utopia. Critics such as Judith Butler (in her book *Gender Trouble*) have seen that Wittig assumes a nostalgic once-upon-a-time social unity, which did not exist, and has never existed. Rather than rewriting or radically challenging notions of gender and sexuality, Wittig's texts affirm heterosexual and homosexual norms (1990, 115, 121). Wittig's view of lesbian sexual-ity and art is problematic: its relations to heteropatriarchy in particular are ambiguous. Wittig's texts, though, despite the confusions, offer an exuberant and thought-provoking revision of the heterosexual establish-ment.

Monique Wittig's lesbian philosophy is radical, in that she claims that lesbians are outside of heterosexual culture, and therefore the term 'woman' does not apply to them. In *Questions Féministes* in 1980, Wittig published an article ("The Straight Mind") which claimed that 'lesbians are not women' (1992, 32).

This form of (theoretical) lesbian separatism provides both a powerful position from which to speak, and an undermining of 'female' or 'women's' power. Being outside the group of (heterosexual) women could mean that it is difficult to change the heteropatriarchal system. For some feminists, one must work *within* the system in order to change it. Being a radical non-'woman' lesbian in Monique Wittig's view may render revolutionary change difficult. Making heterosexuality and men the 'enemy' as a whole, either socially or theoretically, renders some modes of change difficult, or even impossible. Radical lesbian separatism may be a position of power, but it is fraught with theoretical (and social, political, and ideological) difficulties. Wittig does recognize the social angle of oppression ('[i]t is oppression that creates sex and not the contrary', she says [1992, 2]).

Some commentators have over-emphasized the sexual aspect of Monique Wittig's conception of heterosexuality. For example, Judith Butler in *Gender Trouble* has viewed Wittig's system of the binary sexual divide as 'serving the reproductive aims of a compulsory heterosexuality' (1990, 19). For Wittig, however, there is more to heterosexual oppression than sexual desire. There are also the social institutions of marriage and labour. Wittig writes (in 1982):

> The category of sex is the product of a heterosexual society in which men appropriate for themselves the reproduction and production of women and also their physical persons by means of... the marriage contract. (1992, 6)

In her book *Of Woman Born*, Adrienne Rich defines the modern patriarchal family with its

> super-naturalizing of the penis, its division of labour by gender, its emotional, physical and material possessiveness, its ideal of monogamous marriage until death (and its severe penalties for adultery by the wife), the 'illegitimacy' of a child born outside wedlock, the economic dependency of women, the unpaid domestic services of the wife, the obedience of women and children to male authority, the imprinting and continuation of heterosexual roles. (1977)

Monique Wittig challenges conventional forms of the 'feminine' and language by

> not only reveal[ing] the violence done to women (entering language) but also turns the violence back on to language – the body of the text, of the word – and the body in the text. (J. Still, 1993, 24)

Simone de Beauvoir remarked of liberation for women: 'the first thing is work. Then refuse marriage if possible' (M, 147). In Luce Irigaray's view, women, in the psychoanalytic (Freudian/ Lacanian) system, are objects or commodities that are exchanged between men. Freudian œdipalization becomes in fact an economy of female trade between men. The significance of desire in Irigaray's reading of psychoanalytic sexual economy is not as a lack or focussed on particular objects (women), but a circuit of flows and paths, detours and dynamics. In this narcissistic, phallocentric monopoly, women are not the endpoint but the means or carriers of male desire. As it's between men, this sexual economy is homosexual, governed by and for men.

The lesbian is thus a double negative in this social and metaphysical system: as a woman, she is silenced and negated; as a lesbian she disappears completely from the masculinist system of exchange. The lesbian subverts the economy of trade which is founded on the phallus.

Luce Irigaray playfully, ironically and at times bitterly rewrites Sigmund Freud's work. In her reading of Freud's view of lesbianism, for example, Irigaray deconstructs it to show that it is a fetish figure. Freudian 'female homosexuality', according to Irigaray, is a 'hom(m)o-sexualized' person, the woman who has a male desire for the phallic mother. For Irigaray, Freud's lesbian performs a masculine masquerade in order to hide the double lack which is 'projected on to the lesbian body by the anxious gaze of the male voyeur-theorist'.[15] For Irigaray, masculinist views of lesbianism cannot escape from their phallocentric vision. Thus, lesbian *jouissance* is denied, because phallocentric patriarchy cannot envisage erotic pleasure between women that is not mediated by or motivated by male desire. Male ideologies such as Freudian psychoanalysis do not allow for female autoeroticism or homoeroticism. (For example, the regular scenario in porn – a man watching two women make love).

WOMEN AS WITCHES, OUTSIDERS, POETS

In the Neoplatonic, Aristotlean, Renaissance view of the fine art establishment, there is good art and bad art, there is the art of 'taste', 'decency', 'refinement', 'purity' and 'civilization', and there is the vulgar, the uncouth, the disrespectful, the unornamental, the unlearned. In mediæval culture, there is Sacred and Profane Love, drawn from Plato's *Symposium*, and the figures of Venus Vulgaris (Earthly Venus) and Venus Coelestis.

The Heavenly Venus is the one to aspire to, even though the Earthly Venus may be much more exciting. These dichotomies are found throughout art. There is the chaste, passive, motherly Virgin Mary and the sexual, active, lascivious Mary Magdalene.[16] There is good and evil. There is Heaven and Hell.

There is male and female.

Throughout the history of Western culture one comes across the same dualities, in one form or another. The female is clearly on the 'left' side, on the wrong side of the 'right' way. Women are the 'second sex', 'second class citizens': Sherry Ortner points out that there is an opposition between culture and nature, and women are lower down in the male-made hierarchy:

> my thesis is that woman is being identified with – or, if you will, seems to be a symbol of – something that every culture devalues, something that every culture defines as being of a lower order of existence than itself'.[17]

Women are imprisoned, as Hélène Cixous notes, in masculine binary logic, which is the 'classical vision of sexual opposition between men and women', as Verena Conley comments in her book on Cixous (1984, 129). For Luce Irigaray, this duality is called 'the recto-verso structure that shores up common sense' (I, 127). For Julia Kristeva, the sexism of mediæval religion is an adjunct of the exaltation of the Virgin Mary: in *Tales of Love* she writes:

> The image of the Virgin – the woman whose entire body is an emptiness through the paternal word is conveyed – has remarkably subsumed the maternal 'abject', which is so necessarily intrapsychic. Lacking that safety lock, feminine abjection imposed itself upon social represent-ation, causing an actual denigration of women... (TL, 374)

Feminists speak of experiences beyond male control: pregnancy, childbirth, female orgasm, and *jouissance*. Annie Leclerc, perhaps the most 'essentialist' of French feminists, wrote of the orgasmic pleasures (*jouiss-*

ances) of childbirth, menstruation and lactation in her *Parole de femme*.[17]
Julia Kristeva remarked in *About Chinese Women*:

> If a woman cannot be part of the temporal symbolic order except by
> identifying with the father, it is clear that as soon as she shows any sign
> of that which, in herself, escapes such identification and acts differently,
> resembling the dream of the maternal body, she evolves into this 'truth'
> in question. It is thus that female specificity defines itself in patrilinear
> society: woman is a specialist in the unconscious, a witch, a bacchan-
> alian, taking her jouissance in an anti-Apollonian, Dionysian orgy. (K,
> 154)

Like the poet, woman is a shaman, a witch, a magician, moving beyond
the symbolic/ œdipal/ patriarchal order; 'the female is the initiatrix',
wrote Alex Comfort (1979). This is a continuing theme in the writings of
Julia Kristeva. In "The True-Real" ("Le vréel"), she asserted:

> We know...how logic and ontology have inscribed the question of *truth*
> within *judgement* (or sentence structure) and *being*, dismissing as *mad-
> ness, mysticism or poetry* any attempt to articulate that impossible ele-
> ment which henceforth can only be designated by the Lacanian category
> of the *real*. After the flowering of mysticism, classical rationality, first
> by embracing Folly with Erasmus, and then by excluding it with
> Descartes, attempted to enunciate the real as truth by setting limits on
> Madness; modernity, on the other hand, opens up this enclosure in a
> search for other forms capable of transforming or rehabilitating the
> status of *truth*. (K, 217)

Myra Jehlen wonders that, if there is no extra-patriarchal space, can
there be a feminist, non-patriarchal discourse?[17] Feminists such as Elaine
Showalter and Jeanne Roberts, taking their cue from Edwin Ardener,[18]
propose that there is a female 'wild zone', as there is a male 'wild zone'.
One knows about men's version of wild zone eroticism, what Hélène
Cixous calls 'glorious phallic monosexuality' (M, 254). Female 'otherness'
is beyond patriarchal space, beyond patriarchal representations.[19] Showalter in "Feminist Criticism in the Wilderness" suggests that, in terms of
space, the female 'wild zone' 'is literally no-man's land, a place

JULIA KRISTEVA

forbidden to men', while as (an) experience, it refers to aspects of women's life unavailable to or outside of male experience; metaphysically, it may be a space quite outside of masculine consciousness (ib., 262).

✤

Always Luce Irigaray has been concerned with the notion of 'woman' as 'outsider', of the otherness and outsideness of women in a patriarchal regime. The feminine, says Irigaray, 'had to be deciphered as forbidden' (S, 20). In *Speculum of the Other Woman*, Irigaray describes 'woman' as 'off-stage, off-side, beyond representation, beyond self-hood' (22). Irigaray depicts 'woman' as philosophy's 'other', so she is interested in those women who have been 'outsiders' in history – the hysteric, the witch, the mediæval mystic, those people who 'stand outside' culture, using the techniques of ecstasy ('ex-stase', Irigaray spells it, 'ecstasy' meaning, from the Greek, 'stand outside'). Both Irigaray and Julia Kristeva spoke of the special creative positionality of the mediæval women mystics, who occupied the maternal liminal place of the mother, where the object of devotion became less fixed, more open, less dogmatic, more 'feminine'. Kristeva speaks of an ethics of heresy, an 'herethics' or 'herethical ethic'.

For Julia Kristeva, Christianity offers a limited number of ways in which women can participate in the 'symbolic Christian order': for women who are not virgins or nuns, who have orgasms and give birth

> her only means of gaining access to the symbolic paternal order is by engaging in an endless struggle between the orgasmic maternal body and the symbolic prohibition – a struggle that will take the form of guilt and mortification, and culminate in masochistic *jouissance*. For a woman who has not easily repressed her relationship with her mother, participation in the symbolic paternal order as Christianity defines it can only be masochistic. (TL, 147)

Two of the classic ways in which women have been allowed to participate in Christianity is the *'ecstatic* and the *melancholy'* (ib.). According to Elizabeth Grosz in "Lesbian Fetishism?", women can disavow their own castration (*contra* Sigmund Freud) through hysteria – women phallicizing part of their bodies; the 'masculine complex' – women taking the phallus as their love object; and narcissism – women turning their bodies into the phallus (E. Grosz, 1991). As Julia Kristeva put it, 'the lover... reconciles narcissism and hysteria' (TL, 33). Hélène Cixous wrote in "The Laugh of the Medusa" of women as outsiders or witches, living in the unconscious or the wilderness, who must return

> from afar, from always, from "without", from the heath where witches are kept alive; from below, from "beyond" culture... (M, 247)

An outcast or witch, 'woman' may also exist within the traditional economies and languages. In Hélène Cixous' terms, 'woman' must be the darer, the one who 'goes and passes into infinity', the traveller who 'alone wishes to know from within', even though she is eternally the outcast (M, 260).

Julia Kristeva and Luce Irigaray, among other French feminists, have spoken of something in women or the feminine that is 'unrepresentable', beyond art, beyond male culture. 'Woman' is always negative, always outside the symbolic realm; 'woman' 'isn't this (can't be defined), it isn't yet that (isn't yet here)', Claire Duchen noted in *Feminism in France From May '68 to Mitterand* (85).

This notion of 'woman' as 'outsider' is aligned to Julia Kristeva's notion of the *sujet-en-procès* and the 'negativity' of the text, which Kristeva developed in early works such as *Séméiotikè, La Révolution du langage poétique* and *Polylogue*. In *About Chinese Women*, Kristeva writes of the woman as a witch, someone outside of patriarchal discourse, or at least, thrown to the edge, the border between the known and the otherness:

> A *jouissance* which breaks the symbolic chain, the taboo, the mastery. A *marginal discourse*, with regard to the science, religion and philosophy of the *polis* (witch, child, underdeveloped, not even a poet, at best his accomplice). (K, 154)

For Julia Kristeva, feminine *jouissance* relates to the part of women that goes beyond the laws of language and Oedipus. Thus, the woman who exists within œdipal law, must also accept the loss of her *jouissance*.

Sherry Ortner writes that 'woman is being identified with – or, if you will, seems to be a symbol of – something that every culture devalues'.[18] Ann Rosalind Jones describes Kristeva's notion of the 'outsider' culture of women, of women as 'witches':

> Women, for Kristeva... speak and write as "hysterics," as outsiders to male-dominated discourse, for two reasons: 'the predominance in them of drives related to anality and childbirth, and their marginal position *vis-à-vis* masculine culture. Their semiotic style is likely to involve repetitive, spasmodic separations from the dominating discourse, which, more often, they are forced to imitate.[20]

For Alice Jardine, Julia Kristeva's notion of the Other or alterity always ends up with the other sex. The first Other may be the mother, but Kristeva, Jardine maintains, 'has repeatedly pointed out that the Other is always in fact the "other sex"', and in "Opaque Texts" Jardine quotes Kristeva in *Revolution in Poetic Language*: '[t]he difference between 'I' and 'you' turns out to be coextensive with the sexual difference' (Rev, 326). Kristeva's female voice, though, Jardine asserts, is 'strangely sub-versive'.[21]

Julia Kristeva's writings may be the most coherent and incisive account of psycho-cultural 'otherness'. Victor Burgin, describing Kristeva's philosophy, says that she positions

> the woman in society... in the patriarchal, as perpetually at the boundary, the borderline, the edge, the 'outer limit' – the place where order shades into chaos, light into darkness. The peripheral and ambivalent position allocated to woman, says Kristeva, had led to that familiar division of the field of representation in which women are viewed as either saintly or demonic – according to whether they are seen as bringing the darkness, or as keeping it out.[22]

Saintly woman (the Virgin Mary is a typical example) keeps the amazing energy of female otherness out of men's lives; the demonic woman (Mary Magdalene, the *femme fatale*, vampire, 'devil woman') is the one who brings the wildness with her. Patriarchy of course prefers bland, mute, passive door-stops in women, people who will stop the darkness from coming in, who will sit there and say nothing and get on with society's housework.

André Breton said the 'existence is elsewhere'. French feminists say that 'woman' is elsewhere. 'She is indefinitely other in herself,' comments Luce Irigaray in *This Sex Which Is Not One*, maintaining that women

> are already elsewhere than in the discursive machinery where you claim to take them by surprise. They have turned back within themselves, which does not mean the same thing as 'within yourself'. They do not experience the same interiority that you do and which perhaps you mistakenly presume they share. (68-69)

Here, perhaps, is female 'otherness'. Some of the wildness and strangeness and ecstasy of female eroticism may be experienced and depicted. Luce Irigaray also spoke in spatial terms of idealist feminism:

> We need both space and time. And perhaps we are living in an age when *time must re-deploy space*. Could this be the dawning of a new world? Immanence and transcendence are being recast, notably by that *threshold* which has never been examined in itself: the female sex. It is a threshold unto *mucosity*. Beyond the classic opposites of love and hate, liquid and ice lies this perpetually *half-open* threshold, consisting of *lips* that are strangers to dichotomy. Pressed against one another, but without any possibility of suture, at least of a real kind, they do not absorb the world either into themselves or through themselves, provided they are not abused or reduced to a mere consummating or consuming structure. Instead their shape welcomes without assimilating or reducing or devouring. A sort of door unto voluptuousness, then? Not that, either: their useful function is to designate a *place*: the very place of uses, at least on a habitual plane. Strictly speaking, they serve neither conception nor *jouissance*. Is this, then, the mystery of female identity, of its self-contemplation, of that strange word of silence; both the threshold and reception of exchange, the sealed-up secret of wisdom, belief and faith in every truth?[23]

Many feminists suggest that women's eroticism cannot be represented, much as women themselves cannot be represented. Julia Kristeva writes: '[i]n "woman" I see something that cannot be represented, something that is not said, something above and beyond nomenclatures and ideologies.'[24] Other feminists echo this idea, that women cannot be fully represented in the traditional media of patriarchy. As Hélène Cixous commented:

> It is at the level of sexual pleasure in my opinion that the difference makes itself most clearly apparent in as far as woman's libidinal economy is neither identifiable by a man nor referrable to the masculine economy. ("Sorties", M, 95)

The unrepresentable in art and pornography, according to some feminists, is women's eroticism, their *jouissance*, that 'explosive, blossoming, sane and inexhaustible *jouissance* of the woman', as Julia Kristeva described it in *About Chinese Women* (63).

What is found in most Western art, from Greek and Roman sculpture through the glories of the Renaissance to the latest pornography, are male representations of female eroticism. Feminists say that there are no real depictions of female *jouissance* in art or literature. 'In my opinion,' remarked Marguerite Duras, 'women have never expressed themselves.'[25] What she means, perhaps, is that women have expressed themselves thus far in the terms and means defined by men. There is no 'feminine' or 'women's' writing, according to some feminists. For Duras, 'the future belongs to women. Men have been completely dethroned' (M, 238).

Real sex, the French feminists argue, has not yet been represented. Women haven't done it because they work within the same patriarchal structures, codes and constraints as men. Men, generally, haven't got a hope of depicting authentic female eroticism, although the authors of millions of pornographic products would claim they know everything about female eroticism. On the other hand, in the mechanisms of cultural and postmodern theory, anyone, male or female, should be able to create a truly 'feminine' text. It shouldn't matter who the author is. If the French feminists are right, then nearly all of the art produced anywhere is oriented to the male and the masculine, *even* when it is created by *women*. Many women artists would dispute this. The notion of an 'authentic' 'women's'/ 'feminine' art continues to be hotly debated.[26]

Écriture feminine is a subversive position and activity, which decon-structs patriarchal (phallogocentric) language (S. Hekman, 42). The 'soph-isticated theoretical dilemma' of Hélène Cixous's project was whether a 'female' or 'feminine' voice could be envisaged without 'acquiring its own kind of phallocentricity' (J. Duran, 174). If the woman's voice became phallocentric it was as if she had picked up the phallus itself.[27] The fluid, plural and diffuse sense of 'feminine writing' subverts masculine culture.[28]

Luce Irigaray privileges a poetry of women's laughter in the face of phallocracy; both Irigaray and Hélène Cixous advocate intimate, pers-onal, precious languages of imaginary spaces that exist outside of phallo-cracy (L. Kipnis, 207). According to the French feminists, 'women's' or 'feminine' or 'female' art is created in the gaps and silences of a text, but not in the intentional space of the artwork. Mary Jacobus explains:

> The French insistence on *écriture féminine* – on woman as a writing-effect instead of an origin – asserts not the sexuality of the text but the textuality of sex. Gender difference, produced, not innate, becomes a matter of the structuring of a genderless libido in and through patria-rchal discourse. Language itself would at once repress multiplicity and heterogeneity – true difference – by the tyranny of hierarchical oppo-sitions (man/woman) and simultaneously work to overthrow that tyranny by interrogating the limits of meaning. The 'feminine', in this scheme, is to be located in the gaps, the absences, the unsayable or unrepresentable of discourse and representation. (1982, 14, 1)

For some feminists, philosophies based on the body are problematic, because to look for some essential nature of 'woman', some essence based in biology, is dubious.[29] Indeed, Toril Moi says that 'to define 'woman' is necessarily to essentialize her' (1988, 139). Jacques Derrida had written in *Spurs* that

> There is no such thing as the essence of woman because woman averts, she is averted of herself. Out of the depths, endless and unfathomable, she engulfs and distorts all vestige of essentiality, of identity, of prop-erty. (51)

What is 'woman', anyway? A 'writing-effect', for the feminist Alice Jardine, an element in culture or a text. For Julia Kristeva, 'woman' does not 'exist', because there is no 'essence', no 'essential' woman (S. Hekman, 148). For Kristeva, not only 'woman' and the subject is 'in process' (*sujet-en-procès*), but the body and sexuality as well. French feminism produces a feminist 'space' rather than a 'sex'; the position is a cultural one, not, as in Anglo-American feminism, a discourse based on the biological woman. It's important, as Monique Wittig notes, to make a distinction between the various interpretations 'woman' and 'women':

> Our first task... is thoroughly to dissociate "woman" (the class within which we fight) and "woman," the myth. For "woman" does not exist for us; it is only an imaginary formation, while "women" is the duct of a social relationship.[30]

Elaine Showalter writes of the biologic and genderized views of feminism in "Feminist Criticism in the Wilderness":

> Organic or biological criticism is the most extreme statement of gender difference, of a text indelibly marked by the body: anatomy is textuality... Simply to invoke anatomy risks a return to the crude essentialism, the phallic and ovarian theories of art, that oppressed women in the past.[31]

Biology, though, is crucial; the body is crucial.[32] Hélène Cixous states: '[i]n censuring the body, one censures at the same time breathing and speech' (NBW, 179). But feminists such as Elaine Showalter are wary of biologist or essentialist philosophies, especially those of French feminism.[33]

As Simone de Beauvoir put it, women are not born, they are made, meaning socially, culturally, politically, ideologically, psychologically, etc. For de Beauvoir, 'nature plays an infinitesimal role in the development of a human being': instead, it was socialization that made all of the difference; it was everything that happened after birth. Thus, women were neither superior nor inferior to men, there was no 'eternal feminine', and 'a woman has no special value because she is a woman. That would be the most retrograde "biologism", in total contradiction with everything I think' (M, 153). Women are not 'superior' to men for Luce Irigaray: 'why think in quantative terms? They are *different*' (I, 190).

For Suzanne Horer and Jeanne Socquet, there was no point in simply following what men have done. That would mean repeating the same mistakes:

> We must not follow in the footsteps men have imprinted on this earth. Why repeat the same errors with the same too obviously, catastrophic results? We do not believe in social revolutions that aim at "changing man". Such jolts shift problems without ever solving them in depth. (M, 243)

Hélène Cixous, though, rejected the idea of a 'general woman', or a single type of feminine sexuality (in "The Laugh of the Medusa"). She said there was no essence in femininity or masculinity, but that 'everything is language' (in V. Conley, 1984, 57). In *The Newly Born Woman* Cixous and Catherine Clément stated that there is 'no 'nature' or 'essence' as such', but, instead,

> living structures that are caught and sometimes rigidly set within historico-cultural limits so mixed up with the scene of History that for a long time it has been impossible (and it is still very difficult) to think or even imagine an 'elsewhere'... (1986, 83)

Appealing to the body is not necessarily essentialist, as feminists have noted.[34] And bodies do tend to be kinda important, even for hyper-spatial postmodern theorists who'd like to erase everything related to the body.

PART TWO

LOVE, ABJECTION, MELANCHOLY, ART, LOVE: JULIA KRISTEVA'S PHILOSOPHY

4

JULIA KRISTEVA'S QUEST

In her many projects, Julia Kristeva called upon the 'classic' artists of (mainly European) modernism and the *avant garde*: Antontin Artaud, James Joyce, Ferdinand Céline, Georges Bataille, Comte de Lautréamont, and Stephane Mallarmé. (Kristeva has also written of painters, such as in her landmark essays on Giotto and Giovanni Bellini; she has also discussed Jackson Pollock and his relation to the *chora* in a 1989 essay.)[1] Kristeva sees the modern novel as a structure of 'potential infinity' (*Texte du roman*, 75), which recalls D.H. Lawrence's view that one can put anything into a novel, that the novel's the 'bright book of life'.

A few critics have noted the conflicts between Julia Kristeva's post-modern ethics and her enshrinement of the *avant garde* modernists. The application of the semiotic to *avant garde* texts, for example, may be too easy – it could be shown to function in any text. Kristeva may be placing too much emphasis on the artist and the power of artistic production to effect changes. Kristeva's project may be too much reliant on modernist notions of artisthood, which have been altered by the information era of postmodernism. Andreas Huyssen has noted that Kristeva celebrated the negative æsthetics of James Joyce and Stéphane Mallarmé while ignoring a tradition of women's writing. Kristeva's enshrinement of (largely masculine) *avant garde* writers may have helped to exclude considerations of women in high culture.[2]

Julia Kristeva's point, though, was that *avant garde* writing could offer a revolutionary position from which to speak: she argued that each new subject transforms and revolutionizes the subject that came before it. Poetry has a poetic logic which's not that of everyday language, Kristeva said in "Poésie et négativité" (1969); it is not the bivalent logic of the sign, the 0-1 of everyday living (*Séméiotiké*, 258f). Rather, poetic language is fluid, and escapes being nailed down to definitions; it is 'unobservable'.

The semiotic poet, though, has an ambiguous relation with an industrial society, for the semiotic poet dissolves meanings, and regards subjectivity as an 'open system'. Poetic language subverts denotation, verisimilitude and meaning (*Bedeutung*). Poetry as mimesis becomes a transgression of the thetic. Poetry might be able to transform not only the symbolic, on the linguistic level, but also in the social realm (*Revolution in Poetic Language*, 83). The symbolic order in poetry is being continually modified by the semiotic (ib., 62).

The poetic text *à la* Julia Kristeva, Elizabeth Grosz explained in "The Body of Signification",

> materializes the pleasures, rhythms and drives of the semiotic; religious discourse is the site of a privileged symbolic representation of the semiotic, in which the symbolic is able to tolerate the expression of normally unspoken pre-œdipal pleasures. (1990, 99)

In Julia Kristeva's view, poetry is 'capitalist society's carnival, a way of keeping death and madness at bay' (L, 6). The *chora* unleashed is explosive, pulverizing (ib., 103), but the 'revolution' that poetic language brings about must occur within social systems. Kristeva, Griselda Pollock claims, failed to appreciate that modernism's 'revolutions' (against edifices such as the family, the State and religion) actually privileged men in the end.[3] Kristeva's feminist position is somewhere between postmodern philosophy and feminist rewritings of humanism.[4]

For Julia Kristeva, writers such as Antonin Artaud were disturbing, because in them identity was unstable. There was a destabilization of meaning and of the self in these *avant garde* writers, which echoed Kristeva's notion of the fragmentation of the ego and meaning in a post-modernist world. Art is 'open to the other', Kristeva says. Art confronts people with a void of non-meaning, but also offers way in which a rebirth of the self can occur in language (J. Fletcher, 1990, 219).

Among the other things that Sigmund Freud drove a piledriver through was the ego, which has remained shattered ever since Freud. Hélène Cixous, Luce Irigaray and Julia Kristeva all agree on the fragmentation of identity since the endeavours of psychoanalysis. Kristeva writes: a 'fixed identity' is a 'fiction, an illusion – who among us has a 'fixed' identity?' (QS, 129). Kristeva's sense of poetic language dissolves subjectivity so thoroughly the subject becomes a 'paragrammatic space', an 'empty' space, something like the negativity of Buddhist mysticism where 'a "zerologic" subject, a non-subject comes to assume the thought which cancels it out', Kristeva wrote in *Séméiotiké* (273-4). In Kristeva's meta-physical world, fluidity and flux is emphasized. In her interview with Susan Sellers, Kristeva says:

> I wanted to examine the language which manifests these states of instability because in ordinary communication – which is organized, civilized – we repress these states of incandescence. (129)

In *Desire in Language* Julia Kristeva remarked:

> Poetic language, the only language that uses up transcendence and theology to sustain itself; poetic language, knowingly the enemy of religion, by its very economy borders on psychosis (as for its subject) and totalitarianism or fascism (as for the institution it implies or

evokes). (125)

As a student of psychoanalysis and poetry, Julia Kristeva is bound to be interested in exploring marginality, instability, and repression. Indeed, this might be seen as Kristeva's quest, a quest for the experiences and meanings on the edges of society and culture. No wonder that Kristeva looked to poets for an exploration of this marginal realm. The poet and artist is dedicated, in one sense, to an exploration of everything that is suppressed, repressed, obsessed, dispossessed. Poets have long been adventurers of the unconscious – this was a popular view in the years of High Modernism, the years of James Joyce's *Ulysses*, Marcel Proust's *Remembrance of Times Past* and T.S. Eliot's *The Wasteland*.

It is fitting that Julia Kristeva should be interested in poets and writers who create the ubiquitous modernist 'stream of consciousness' writing. For Kristeva, 'stream of unconsciousness' is a more fitting term. It is here, in the zone called 'wild' by some feminists, or called the 'underworld' in Classic mythology, that poets go. The underworld is their creative space. Kristeva's point is that these states and zones are continually margin-alized, or made 'abject'.

And they are rich – *so rich*. Yes. Listen: the key ancestor in this journey into the underworld is of course Orpheus, and it's no coincidence that most of the poets and artists that Julia Kristeva, Hélène Cixous and Luce Irigaray enshrine are Orphic poets (Antonin Artaud, Stéphane Mallarmé, James Joyce, Arthur Rimbaud, Rainer Maria Rilke). The Orphic poet is intensely lyrical, fluid and open, like Friedrich Hölderlin, Novalis, Rimbaud, Sappho: these are Orphic poets. The Orphic poet is also of course an outsider, which is a personality or (arche)type that concerns Kristeva deeply. At times, Kristeva will speak of the poet, but when she does one can insert witch, or shaman, or outsider.[4] In "Baudelaire, or Infinity, Perfume, and Punk", Kristeva speaks ironically of the outsider status of the artist in a bourgeois society which offers no refuge:

> If through a writing that is synonymous with the amatory condition – an experience at the limits of the identifiable – the writer can find no

other place in the bosom of bourgeois society than that of a refugee at the side of nonproductive nobility or of the Church, which protects fetishes under the symbolic umbrella, we can only interpret that as an indictment of that very society rather than the evidence of the writer's error or "failure". (TL, 339)

The idea of the 'Orphic poet' is essentially shamanic: for, beyond the ancient, mythic figure of Orpheus is the figure of the archaic shaman, who is the witch doctor, the dancing sorcerer, the angelic traveller to other worlds who brings back news of goings-on in the transcendent realm. The shaman (who in the myths is called Orpheus, Isis or Jesus) travels into the Underworld and manages to return. This is her/ his special shamanic technique: the ability to die *and* return. S/he is a master of ecstasy, as Mircea Eliade said, and the ecstatic state is largely one of rebirth. The archaic shaman goes into a hypnotic trance and flies to other worlds, sometimes escorting dead souls to the Other World. But the 'other world', as poets know well, is simply this world – only more so.[5] It is this other world that Kristeva investigates. And what illuminates the other world is precisely the 'states of incandescence' of the poets. But this incandescence which so vividly lights up the dark, repressed realm, is dependent upon artistic suffering and instability. Kristeva writes:

we repress these states of incandescence. Creativity as well as suffering comprises these moments of instability, where language, or the signs of language, or subjectivity itself are put into 'process'. And one can extrapolate this notion and use it not just for the texts of Artaud but for every 'proceeding' in which we move outside the norms. (QS, 129)

Again, the shamanic journey of the outsider or *baccanale* or witch is hinted at here: when 'we move outside the norms'. The people Julia Kristeva points to, again and again, are the ones who 'move outside the norms'. They are the ones, after all, who help to show where the norms are, where the borders are between sanity and madness, fantasy and reality, inner and outer, representation and identity, stability and instability.

> Since at least Hölderlin [she writes], poetic language has deserted beauty and meaning to become a laboratory where, facing philosophy, knowledge, and the transcendental ego of all signification, the imposs-ibility of a signified or signifying identity is being sustained. If we took this venture seriously – if we could hear the burst of black laughter it hurls at all attempts to master the human situation, to master language by language – we would be forced to re-examine 'literary history', to rediscover beneath rhetoric and poetics its unchanging but always different polemic with the symbolic function. (DL, 145)

Let's get back to the young artist (or individual): that is, to those primal and primary zones of the womb, fluids, the maternal, the first few months of existence outside of the mother. For Julia Kristeva, the artist activates the tensions between the realms of the symbolic and the semiotic, between expression and repression, between the maternal and the individual. In the first stages of differentiation, identity is still shaky, and the individual confuses her/ himself with the maternal image. The way out of this confusion, in the classic scenario, is via the age-old œdipal triangle. The (male) child must split up his mother in order to take up his masculine gender: she is split into the abject and the sublime Kristeva says in her *Powers of Horror* (PH, 157). Abjecting the mother enables the child to separate himself from the mother. To counter the mother becoming a phobic object, if she is only abjected, the phobic substitutes a sign for the absent object (PH, 45). Abjection thus operates in an in-between zone, as Kristeva calls it, 'of phobia, obsessions, and perversion' (ib.). Her defin-ition of abjection is striking: 'the abject is the violence of mourning for an "object" that has always already been lost'.

A loving 'imaginary' father is necessary for this journey through the stages of Kristevan abjection: the imaginary constructs encourage the separation from the mother. Only when the child identifies with the space opened up by the archaic or imaginary father, the paternal space, 'the father of individual pre-history' (TL, 26), can narcissism occur. Love always involves separation in Kristeva's psychology of the individual.

The phobic discourse relates to the artist directly, for writers are among those most enmeshed in grappling with a fear of the void: '[t]he writer is a phobic who succeeds in metamorphizing in order to keep from being frightened to death; instead he comes to life again in signs' (PH, 38). Art, for Julia Kristeva, creates both the subject and the object, it is the 'possibility of fashioning narcissism and of subtilizing the ideal' (*Histoires d'Amour*, 1984, 21).

All this leads to one of Julia Kristeva's most provocative ideas, that of the *chora* and the semiotic modality, which was so eloquently explored in *Révolution du langage poétique*, one of Kristeva's key theoretical texts. For Kristeva, the *chora* is an archaic pre-œdipal space, linked to the semiotic modality, a realm of uncertainty, undetermined articulation, ambiguity. It occurs in a phase of mother-child *jouissance* and polymorphous perversity, a time of rhythmic, heterogeneous impulses before the child enters the Symbolic realm. The *chora* is the place where the subject is generated and negated. The sounds associated with the semiotic realm include laughter and word-games, the voice seen as rhythm and tone, and the body in its motion and rhythm. The word *chora* means receptacle in Greek, Kristeva explains. In chapter two of *Revolution in Poetic Language*, "The Semiotic *Chora* Ordering the Drives", Kristeva writes:

> We borrow the term *chora* from Plato's *Timaeus* to denote an essentially mobile and extremely provisional articulation constituted by movements and their ephemeral stases. We differentiate this uncertain and indeterminate *articulation* from a *disposition* that already depends on representation, lends itself to phenomenological, spatial intuition and gives rise to a geometry. (K, 93)

Note that Julia Kristeva is at pains to stress that the *chora* is a mobile, provisional concept: 'extremely provisional', she says. In introducing the idea of the *chora*, Kristeva knows that it will cause some misinterpretations, so she freights her thesis with footnotes on Plato and space. Kristeva explains that her reading of Plato acknowledges the space or receptacle or *chora* as simultaneously and ambiguously a 'real' and an imaginary space, at once conceptual and amorphous. In *Polylogue* Kristeva defines the *chora* thus: 'Plato's *Timaeus* speaks of a *chora*, receptacle, unnamable, improbable, hybrid, anterior to naming, to the One, to the father' (DL, 133).

Critics have seized on Julia Kristeva's semiotic and *chora*, solidifying it in academic prose, but Kristeva's own explanation of the *chora* in *La Révolution du langage poétique* emphasizes ambiguity and the non-representable. She comes at the *chora* via the not-this not-that of Oriental philosophy, defining it by what it is *not*: it is not a sign, nor a position, not a model, nor a copy, and it precedes figuration and specularization (K, 94).

The poet, in a sense, writes inside the mother, or from the mother, or from the maternal realm. 'The poet's *jouissance* that causes him to emerge from schizophrenic decorporealization is the *jouissance* of the mother', writes Kristeva (1986, 192). But why, Kristeva asks, 'is the speaking subject incapable of uttering the mother within her very self? Why is it that the "mother herself" does not exist?' And why, Kristeva adds, is the mother only phallic? (*Desire in Language*, 194).

The semiotic activity which's expressed in poetic language is a mark, Julia Kristeva writes, of drives such as life/ death, love/ hate, appropriation/ rejection, orality/ anality (DL, 136). Poetic language leads back to the mother, to primal incest, to the exchange of women in society:

Language as symbolic function constitutes itself at the cost of repressing instinctual drive and continuous relation to the mother. On the contrary, the unsettled and questionable subject of poetic language (for whom the word is never uniquely sign) maintains itself at the cost of reactivating this repressed instinctual, maternal element. If it is true that the prohibition of incest constitutes, at the same time, language as communicative code and women as exchange objects in order for a society to be established, *poetic language would be* for its questionable subject-in-process the *equivalent of incest*: it is within the economy of signification itself that the questionable subject-in-process appropriates to itself this archaic, instinctual, and maternal territory; thus it simultaneously prevents the word from becoming mere sign and the mother from becoming an object like any other – forbidden. (DL, 136)

There is something inevitably nostalgic about Julia Kristeva's evocation of the semiotic realm, for the semiotic mode 'bears the most archaic memories of our link with the maternal body' (QS, 130). For some feminists, this is where the richness of the *chora* and the *semiotic* stems from: for the semiotic modality is associated with the pre-œdipal maternal realm, a powerful psychological space, associated with the mother-child dyad.

One can see how this reactivation of primal, apparently nostalgic modalities is troubling for some feminists. Julia Kristeva seems to be avoiding the problems of history and society, substituting history for carnival, as one critic reckoned.6 In books such as *About Chinese Women, In the Beginning Was Love, Tales of Love* and *Language, the Unknown,* Kristeva has shown she is very much concerned with history, materialism and societies.

Julia Kristeva's *chora* is a suitably 'postmodern' concept, with its aspects of ambiguity, fragmentary nature, ambivalent relation to identity, and so on. It seems an appropriate concept for the age which Michel Foucault characterizes as founded on 'the void made by man's dis-appearance' and Fredric Jameson calls 'hyperspace', a space that trans-cends the human body.7

This Jamesonian 'hyperspatiality' corresponds to another postmodern concept, the non-place of the (American) desert of key French theorist Jean Baudrillard.8 This non-place or void is created by a 'crisis of the master's discourse',9 In the non-place or hyperspatial void, words are unwelcome. ('Words, even when they speak of the desert, are always unwelcome', quipped Baudrillard [ib., 71]). In the empty space of the *chora*, Jacques Derrida said, one can 'avoid speaking'.10

It is precisely the relation between the *chora* and speaking and art that interests Julia Kristeva (art is 'the semiotization of the symbolic', Kristeva says [R, 79]). Or it is one of the most intriguing relations in Kristeva's mythopœia. Kristeva, though, does not do away with the speaking subject, as Jacques Derrida does: '[w]riting can never be thought under the category of the subject', wrote Derrida in *Of Grammatology* (68).

Other relations to Julia Kristeva's *chora* include the philosophy of Martin Heidegger. One recalls not only Heidegger's notions of being, presence and time, but also his 'abyss' (*Abgrund*) or 'groundless ground'[11] and the 'clearing' (after Plato).[12] Echoing Heidegger, Kristeva has linked the *chora* to Heidegger's notion of 'chaos', a term which Heidegger thought was etymologically associated with *chora*.[13] Jacques Derrida too has expressed his interest in Heidegger's response to (the) *chora*.[14]

Julia Kristeva valued the term 'anaphora' in linguistics, which relates to the chaos of the *chora*. Anaphora describes the link between language and what is outside language; it is the 'non-spoken', the 'silent and mute', the 'non-written', the 'non-structured'. Instead of the sign existing in stasis outside of material practice, anaphora emphasizes the connections between language and materiality (the body), between words and flesh.

As an aside, one of Julia Kristeva's more dubious notions in linguistics is of the child's first morphemes, or sounds, which Kristeva sees as related to the instinctive oral and anal drives: in words such as 'mama' and 'papa' (in French), Kristeva finds the phoneme /m/ which relates to sucking, and /p/ which's explosive or 'anal'.

5

❀

THE PSYCHOLOGY OF THE ARTIST IN JULIA KRISTEVA'S PHILOSOPHY

For Julia Kristeva, as for Sigmund Freud and Jacques Lacan who tackled the experiences of birth and growth before her, something extraordinary happens in the stages of early growth. Kristeva's outsider artist is sited somewhere between Oedipus and Orpheus, the symbolic and the semiotic. In the 'semiotic' phase, all is flux and incoherence, provisional, inchoate, occasional.[1] It is a pre-linguistic mode, anterior to syntax, denotation and meaning, Kristeva explained in *Desire In Language*. Then, with the mirror phase and the castration in the Oedipus complex, the individual is enculturated and civilized – language is acquired, and articulation. Importantly, the symbolic is a phase of identification. The symbolic links to the father, to the Law of the Father, the Lacanian *nom/ non du père* ('name/ no of the father'), to symbolic laws, to patriarchal power, to sign, syntax, and social constraints (DL, 6-7).

> The maternally defined semiotic is the prop or support of, as well as the site for, the disruptive transgression of the paternal, patriarchally regulated Symbolic.

writes Elizabeth Grosz (1992, 195). The semiotic cannot be circumscribed by the symbolic order; it is always threatening to disrupt it. Even though one enters the symbolic, however, the semiotic is never wholly eliminated. Subjectivity still includes some aspect of the otherness, the alien, marginal and repressed realm.[2] Indeed, some artists deliberately encourage the relationship with the semiotic.

One of Julia Kristeva's more intriguing ideas is that artistic creation is perhaps linked with the 'infantile babblings' of the archaic semiotic modality.[3] For Kristeva, art and artistic creation may have an archaic element that would unsettle many if they realized it was there consciously. Unconsciously, they know it is so. Witness the archaic pleasures of touching a sculpture, or enjoying the acres of crimson in an abstract painting. Art activates these simple pleasures but critical discourse disguises them as something cerebral, dry, scholarly, distanced, theorized. Whether one sees the experience of the art object as a reuniting with the maternal phallus, or the lost mirror image, or the *objet a*, or the original fetish, the emotions evoked are very powerful. Sometimes the presentation in art of the artwork *as* itself can draw attention to the semiotic or presymbolic – the poem *as* poem, the film *as* film.

Of course, Julia Kristeva's notion that art is born from archaic, seemingly 'simple' pleasures is nothing new. Long before Herr Freud people had known that. What is new in Kristeva's project is the individual and highly poetic way she links the archaic, maternal modality to artistic creation. This is important for feminists, for the phallus, though not absent from Kristeva's *chora* and semiotic, is at least secondary to the archaic womb-space or receptacle. At least the archaic (art) object is not automatically associated in Kristeva's system with the phallus or fæces (Jacques Lacan or Sigmund Freud).

Julia Kristeva founds her philosophy of the *chora* not on the primacy of the phallus as 'transcendent signifier', as in the Lacanian system. (The symbolic is phallic, but has to make itself 'genital' so that sexual difference can be understood [R, 457]). For Lacan, the phallus is the signifier of absence, which is linked with death (this sign also evokes life). Lacan's symbolic may also be a sign of death. For Kristeva, there is a sublimation of maternal *jouissance*:

> At that point we witness the possibility of creation, of sublimation. I think that every type of creation, even if it's scientific, is due to this possibility of opening the norms, towards pleasure, which refers to an archaic experience with a maternal pre-object. (QS, 131)

From the *chora* and semiotic, then, flows poetry. This is where things get very interesting. Artistic creation becomes a struggle involving signific-ation, transgression, the semiotic and the symbolic.⁴ The semiotic is revolutionary because of the way in which the psychological subject has been made up since the Enlightenment: the semiotic can be a means of transgressing the (masculine) symbolic (S. Hekman, 149).

> And so, according to psychoanalysis, poets as individuals fall under the category of fetishism [writes Kristeva]; the very practice of art necessitates reinvesting the maternal *chora* so that it trangresses the symbolic order...the poetic function therefore converges with fetishism; it is not, however, identical to it. What distinguishes the poetic function from the fetishist mechanism is that it maintains a *signification* (*Bedeutung*). All its paths into, indeed valorizations of, pre-symbolic semiotic stases not only require the ensured maintenance of this signification but also serve signification, even when they dislocate it. No text, no matter how 'musicalized', is devoid of meaning or signific-ation; on the contrary, musicalization pluralizes meanings. We may say therefore that the text is not a fetish. (K, 115-6)

Julia Kristeva's description of the 'writer' is quite different from that imagined by newspaper columnists working for the middlebrow Sunday supplements, or visitors to the local public library:

> I shall term "writer" that ability to rebound whereby the violence of
> rejection, in extravagant rhythm, find its way into a multiplied signifier.
> It is not the reconstruction of an unwary subject, reminiscing, in
> hysterical fashion, about his lacks in meaning, his plunges into an
> underwater body. It is rather the return of the limit-as-break, cast-
> ration, and the bar separating signifier from signified, which found
> naming, codification, and language; they do this not in order to vanish
> at that point (as communal meaning would have it), but in order,
> lucidly and consciously, to reject and multiply them, to dissolve even
> their boundaries, and to use them again. (DL, 187)

Always one returns to questions of women's 'otherness', 'difference'
and their ability to form a 'feminine' or 'feminist' ethics or poetics. The
same questions arise: how do women write? How does their art relate to
the maternal, the symbolic, the semiotic? Does the masculine model of
separation from the maternal body and the entry into the symbolic realm
apply completely to women? How much ideology or repression is built
into such a (post-Freudian/ Lacanian psychoanalytic) model?

Julia Kristeva is much concerned with the body and its relation to
language and speaking. The body is the 'outside' in conventional
linguistics: one of Kristeva's projects in her linguistic and semiotic explorations was to reconsider the body and its significance in the production of
expressive language. The body could not be ignored in semiotics,
according to Kristeva, because it was where language was produced.
What was more problematic, though, was how the body appeared in
communication: inseparable as it was from representation, the body could
not be represented, or it appeared in language in a manner similar to the
'arche-trace' in the writing of Jacques Derrida, or it was present
'anaphorically' (J. Lechte, 1990a, 99). One of Kristeva's more provocative
notions, which became central to French feminism, was the co-existence of
body and textuality.

It is no good remaining in the semiotic modality however, much as one
might like to: one would not have a position or social signification from

which to speak. No, one must enter the symbolic realm. If one does not enter the symbolic realm, psychosis may result. In order to create a 'women's' or 'feminist' poetics, one must enter the patriarchal symbolic modality, Julia Kristeva suggests, otherwise one cannot really speak at all. The question then becomes how can the patriarchal and œdipal slant of the symbolic realm be appropriated and turned to 'women's' or 'feminist' goals and expressions?

For Julia Kristeva, the revolutionary role of women today may consist of cultivating a poetics of the marginal and unspoken, of speaking from the interstices and margins in order to maintain a revolutionary stance, but not being an out-and-out rebel, someone who does not confront and integrate the symbolic and the patriarchal. Instead, in *Des Chinoises*, Kristeva suggests that women listen to the unspoken, emphasizing 'at each point what remains unsatisfied, repressed, new, eccentric, incomprehensible' (K, 156). In this way the social establishment may be disturbed, even subverted.

In her far-reaching essay on Giovanni Bellini and Renaissance art, Julia Kristeva describes the relationship between the marginality of the maternal and the artistic enterprise:

> The language of art, too, follows (but differently and more closely) the other aspect of maternal *jouissance*, the sublimation taking place at the very moment of primal repression within the mother's body, arising perhaps unwittingly out of her marginal position. At the intersection of sign and rhythm, of representation and light, of the symbolic and the semiotic, the artist speaks from a place where she is not, where she knows not. (ib, 242)

The artist has to make the ungraspable graspable, as Kristeva notes:

> The artist, as servant of the maternal phallus, displays this always and everywhere unaccomplished art of reproducing bodies and spaces as graspable, masterable objects, within reach of his eye and hand. (DL, 246)

Sacrifice takes its place in Kristevan semiotics as the thetic moment which separates the semiotic from the symbolic. Sacrifice does not, though, let violence loose; rather, it helps to regulate it. When sacrifice is incorporated into religion, violence may be dissipated completely.

The sculpted object is indeed the erotic object *par excellence* in art. It is the phallus endlessly caressed by the eyes, in Lacanian, scopic, scopophillic, voyeuristic pleasure. As Julia Kristeva says, 'isn't art the fetish *par excellence*, one that badly camouflages its archeology?' (R, 115)

On one level, artistic creation counters Lacanian lack and Kristevan absence: the act of writing staves off emptiness and loneliness by filling up the psychic space. As Julia Kristeva wrote in "Freud and Love: Treatment and Its Discontents":

> If narcissism is a defence against the emptiness of separation, then the whole contrivance of imagery, representations, identifications and projections that accompany it on the way towards strengthening the Ego and the Subject is a means of exorcising that emptiness. (TL, 42)

In her psychoanalyst mode, Julia Kristeva reckons that art is born out of the pain of loss. She asserts:

> the creative act is released by an experience of depression without which we could not call into question the stability of meaning or the banality of expression. A writer must at one time or another have been in a situation of loss – of ties, of meaning – in order to write. (QS, 133)

In this intriguing reading of the artistic act, Julia Kristeva presents the artist not as a 'technician of ecstasy', as Mircea Eliade called the archaic shaman, but as a technician of melancholia. The people on the edge – hysterics, obsessionals, lovers, artists – are often sufferers of depression. Underlying many of the complaints of our time, Kristeva said in 1986, is depression (QS, 133). Writing may be one way in which the writer writes her/ his way out of depression.

Certainly one can look to many more writers than the ones Julia Kristeva puts forward (Fyodor Dostoievsky, Gérard de Nerval, Marguerite Duras), to see this counter-depression at work. The angst-ridden artist may be a cliché of our times (Vincent van Gogh, Mark Rothko, Ludwig van Beethoven, Thomas Hardy), but it also fits the facts.

In *Soleil Noir,* Julia Kristeva developed her psychoanalysis of melancholy. For Kristeva, the melancholic is reduced to one basic meaning – despair and pain (*douleur*), rather than a search for meaning. The melancholic fails to develop a sense of the imaginary and symbolic. The inability to mobilize the imaginary and symbolic in the melancholic makes melancholia a kind of living death. Kristevan melancholia is not neurosis, for melancholia does not eroticize the death drive, which results in hatred, and melancholia prevents an eroticization of the separation from the mother. The mother is not the lost object – instead, the subject dies in her place. The artist, though, is able to deal with states such as melancholia because s/he can control signs. The artwork, Kristeva suggests, can be the mark of a 'vanquished depression' (BS, 76).

John Lechte, discussing Julia Kristeva's concept of melancholia, points out that the depressive person is still able to use signs, has not become dissociated from language, but that language 'is always foreign, never material', that language has become detached from energy drives, and emotions have become 'separated from symbolic constructions'. So that Kristevan melancholia is 'the reverse of love with its synthesis of idealization and affect'. For Lechte, 'melancholia is considered by Kristeva to be the equivalent of a mourning for a partial loss which cannot be symbolized. The individual is that loss, weighed down by tears and silence' (1990b, 34-35).

✣

The flipside of the empowering notion of the *chora* in the role of the artist is abjection: Julia Kristeva sees the artist's project as the purifying of abjection. Abjection lies behind the history of religions: the abject is simultaneously the 'land of oblivion' and that 'veiled infinity', the moment 'when revelation bursts forth', Kristeva remarked in *Powers of Horror* (PH, 9). For Kristeva, sociality and subjectivity are founded on abjection, on the expulsion of the unclean and the disorderly. But the abject can never be totally eliminated, and accompanies, in sublimated form, society. The abject is the borderland of ambiguity, a total subjectivity. Ironically, it is *jouissance* that 'alone causes the abject to exist as such. One does not know it, one does not desire it, one joys in it. Violently and painfully. A passion' (PH, 9). The abject is a 'space of simultaneous pleasure and danger', commented Elizabeth Grosz (1990, 94).

Food, urine, vomit, tears and saliva are the things that create abjection – associated with the orifices and body surfaces which become later the erotic zones. Abjection is linked to the body's waste fluids, to those materials which produce disgust (spit, shit, mucus, blood). The fluids of abjection remind society of the body's limitations, its boundaries, its cycles and fatality. These excremental products signify 'the danger to identity that comes from without' (PH, 71).

The subject, in abjection, is never distinct from the objects of abjection. The abject is neither inside nor outside (like the skin on milk), neither dead nor alive (like the corpse). The abject relates to the insecurity of the body image noted Elizabeth Grosz (1992, 198). Menstrual blood, however, indicates a different kind of fear, to do with fecundity and the subject's refusal to recognize the 'corporeal link to the mother' (E. Grosz, 1990, 92).

In her pre-œdipal, semiotic incarnation, the mother is the phallic mother; as the post-œdipal or symbolic mother, she is castrated; the woman who is not or doesn't want to be a mother is seen as suffering from a masculinity complex (ib., 94). The abject, though, is not an object, not something that can be named, not something assimilable, not something definable. The abject is not the Other, nor is it otherness; it is not, either, the subject's correlative. The only quality that the abject has is that it is opposed to the 'I', the subject. The abject worries, nags, seduces desire; yet it cannot be assimilated, so desire rejects it. Even so, there is an impetus or spasm, a leap that is made 'towards an elsewhere as tempting as it is condemned', as Kristeva put it in *Powers of Horror* (PH, 1).

As Elizabeth Grosz points out in "The Body of Signification", the abject aspects of society don't go away: rather,

> it is impossible to exclude the threatening or anti-social elements with any finality. They recur and threaten the subject not only in those events

Freud described as the 'return of the repressed' – that is, in psychical symptoms – they are also a necessary accompaniment of sublimated and socially validated activities, such as the production of art, liter-ature, and knowledges, as well as socially unacceptable forms of sexual drives. (1990, 87)

For Elizabeth Grosz (in "The Body of Signification"), naming the abject 'established a distance or space which may keep its dangers at bay. To speak of the object is to protect oneself against it while at the same time relying on its energetic resources' (1990, 93)

✤

The fluids that Luce Irigaray and Julia Kristeva have appropriated in their form of sexual discourse are the fluids of the 'mother-body' (womb and birth fluids, menstrual blood, breast milk). The fluids of ejaculation have been handed over to masculinist discourse and the male body.4 Female ejaculation is rendered 'invisible' in the dominant (masculinist) discourse, and even lesbian, queer and radical feminisms ignore it. It's much easier, and better, for patriarchal discourse to suppress forms of female sexuality such as female ejaculation, clitoral sex, lesbian sex, and so on, and to keep the primary metaphor for womanhood firmly maternal. This is the way patriarchal economy prefers to render female sexuality – in terms of motherhood, or 'compulsory heterosexuality'. It supports the patriarchal/ masculinist status quo.

The different means of purifying the abject becomes the history of religions in Julia Kristeva's view (PH, 17). For the monotheic religions, abjection persists as taboo or exclusion, associated with defilement and pollution. When the abject encounters Christianity it becomes 'a threat-ening otherness – but always nameable, always totalizeable' (PH, 17). Out of the encounter with the sacred, the abject is written by the artist: art continues the work that religion does, and art will continue, when religion finally dies, to do this catharsis. Kristeva wrote:

In a world in which the Other has collapsed, the æsthetic task – a descent into the foundations of the symbolic construct – amounts to retracting the fragile limits of the speaking being, closest to its dawn, to

the bottomless "primacy" constituted by primal repression. Through
that experience, which is nevertheless managed by the Other, "subject"
and "object" push each other away, confront each other, collapse, and
start again – inseparable, contaminated, condemned, at the boundary
of what is assimilable, thinkable. Great modern literature unfolds over
that terrain: Dostoyevsky, Lautréamont, Proust, Artaud, Kafka, Céline.
(PH, 18)

Julia Kristeva's abject has a Lacanian subtext: it relates to Lacan's lack
and *objet a*: '[t]he abject is the violence of mourning for an "object" that has
always already been lost' (PH, 15).

6

JULIA KRISTEVA AND PAINTING

In the finest reading of the psychology of Giovanni Bellini's art around, Julia Kristeva's "Motherhood According to Bellini", Kristeva makes many points which apply not only to Bellini and other Renaissance painters such as Fra Angelico, Sandro Botticelli, Piero della Francesca and Leonardo da Vinci, but also to the whole artistic project. Kristeva discusses the portrayal of the maternal body in Bellini's (and Renaissance) art. In Kristeva's reading of Renaissance philosophy, the woman is simultaneously allowed to be and not to be the mother; she is placed centrally and simultaneously decentred; she is exalted by painters even as she is denigrated. In Kristeva's semiotic theory, it is artists, almost more than anyone else, who recognize the importance of the *chora*, of the unrepresentable body (the mother):

...craftsmen of Western art reveal better than anyone else the artist's debt to the maternal body and/or motherhood's entry into symbolic existence – that is, translibidinal *jouissance*, eroticism taken over by the language of art. Not only is a considerable portion of pictorial art devoted to motherhood, but within this representation itself, from Byzantine iconography to Renaissance humanism and the worship of the body that it initiates, two attitudes toward the maternal body emerge, prefiguring two destinies within the very economy of Western representation. Leonardo da Vinci and Giovanni Bellini seem to exemplify in the best fashion the opposition between these two attitudes. On the one hand, there is a tilting toward the body as fetish. On the other, a predominance of luminous, chromatic differences beyond and despite corporeal representation. Florence and Venice. Worship of the figurable, representable man; or integration of the image accomplished in its truthlikeness within the luminous serenity of the unrepresentable. ("Motherhood According to Bellini", DL, 243)

In her outstanding essay on the Virgin Mary, "Stabat Mater", Julia Kristeva commented:

Mary's function as guardian of power, later checked when the church became wary of it, nevertheless persisted in popular and pictural representation, witness Piero della Francesca's impressive painting, *Madonna della Misericordia,* which was disavowed by Catholic authorities at the time. And yet, not only did the papacy revere more and more the christly mother as the Vatican's power over cities and municipalities was strengthened, it also openly identified its own institution with the Virgin: Mary was officially proclaimed Queen by Pius XII in 1954 and *Mater Ecclesiae* in 1964. (K, 170)

Against science, in the Renaissance, there is religion. The Madonna presides over the religious domain. Julia Kristeva writes:

There is Christian theology (especially canonical theology); but theology defines maternity only as an impossible elsewhere, a sacred beyond, a vessel of divinity, a spiritual tie with the virginal and committed to assumption.

The Madonna is the primal Mother of all, and Her body is the site of so many conflicting feelings. She is both the giver and taker of life, the desired and the loathed object of desire.[1] In the Dormition or Death of the Virgin, She becomes a little girl in the arms of Her son who is also Her father: the roles are reversed, and She becomes a daughter. She is mother *and* daughter, as well as the *wife*: She 'actualizes the threefold meta-morphosis of a woman in the tightest parenthood structure', Kristeva writes in "Stabat Mater" (K, 169). 'Her replete body, the receptacle and guarantor of demands', remarked Kristeva, 'takes the place of all narcissistic, hence imaginary, effects and gratifications; she is, in other words, the phallus' (R, 101). The Virgin Mary provides a focus for the non-verbal, for those drives and significations which are part of earlier, more archaic processes (M. Jacobus, 1986, 169). The Madonna is the Renaissance version of the 'phallic Mother', site of childhood bliss, site of childhood anxiety. Kristeva writes:

> The face of his [Bellini's] Madonnas are turned away, intent on some-thing else that draws their gaze to the side, up above, or nowhere in particular, but never centres it in the baby. (DL, 247)

Giovanni Bellini's Madonnas present a *jouissance* of maternal space that is, Julia Kristeva noted, 'beyond discourse, beyond narrative, beyond psychology, beyond lived experience and biography' (247). But the Kristevan mother also enables artistic creation, or as Mary Jacobus puts it, '[t]he discourse of maternity gives birth to Kristevan poetics' (1986, 170). Renaissance Madonnas are eroticized through selective parts of the body. One does not see the Virgin naked, ever. One sees, in fact, only Her face and hands, sometimes Her neck. Her body is always covered up. And not just loosely covered, but thickly, heavily covered, heaped up with azure and crimson robes, dresses, wimples and hoods.

Every Renaissance painter had to learn how to paint folds in clothes, and Giovanni Bellini spends a good deal of time and effort producing deep, shadowy folds, 'the luminous folds and secret depths of the sacred', as Julia Kristeva calls them (260). These folds are themselves part of the overall eroticization of the Virgin, and of motherhood. Unable to paint the body of the Mother of God, Renaissance painters threw themselves into painting Her face and hands, and Her clothes. The Madonna's wardrobe is always rich, always indicative of profusion and luxury. The Blessed Virgin Mary is the mother the painter always wanted: quiet, subdued, passive, nurturing, enfolding the child in swathes of love and connection, symbolized by the arms and hands around the child, and those luxuriant robes. Bellini concentrated on creating luminous folds, with deep shadows – in his *Frari Altarpiece* (Venice), for instance, or in the *Madonna and Child with Saints and Donor* (in Düsseldorf).

The folds in the Virgin's mantle are a way of painting the power of the Virgin without revealing Her body, the body which has to be absent, as Julia Kristeva explained in "Motherhood According To Giovanni Bellini":

> The image of the Virgin – the woman whose entire body is an emptiness through which the paternal word is conveyed – had remarkably subsumed the maternal "abject," which is so necessarily intrapsychic.

Julia Kristeva reads Giovanni Bellini's art as a secret autobiography in which the artist tried to displace the father and site himself within the maternal body, to 'rewrite' the body of the mother in his own fashion.

> Giovanni [Bellini] wanted to surpass his father, within the very space of the lost-unrepresentable-forbidden *jouissance* of a hidden mother, seducing the child through a lack of being... He aspired to become the very space where father and mother meet... Bellini penetrates through the being and language of the father to position himself in the place where the mother could have been reached. He thus makes evident this always-already past conditional of the maternal function, which stands instead of the *jouissance* of both sexes. A kind of incest is then committed, a kind of possession of the mother, which provides motherhood, that mute border, with a language; although in doing so, he deprives it of any right to a real existence (there is nothing "feminist" in Bellini's action), he does accord it a symbolic status. (DL, 248-9)

Not 'feminist', then, Giovanni Bellini's paintings in fact uphold every stereotype of 'woman' and 'motherhood' one cares to imagine. In fact, Bellini does not question stereotypes at all: he maintains them. He depicts the Madonna as the drudge of humanity, the drudge as Goddess. Bellini's Madonna is really a mask, too, of something that remains always out-of-reach. The Madonna, as Kristeva notes, 'increasingly appears as a module, a process' (ib., 264).

7

※

JULIA KRISTEVA'S THEORY OF LOVE

Love is the time and space in which "I" assumes the right to be
extraordinary.

Julia Kristeva, "In Praise of Love" (in TL, 5)

One of my favourite books by Julia Kristeva is her *Histoires d'amour*
(1983, translated as *Tales of Love*, 1987). In this book Kristeva embarks
upon a hugely enjoyable tour of the highpoints of Western culture, evolving
an 'ethics of desire' and love founded on the experience of psychoanalytic
transference (as also in *Au commencement était l'amour* [*In the Beginning
Was Love*]). She looks at the *Bible*, the Virgin Mary, and Christian authors

such as Bernard of Clairvaux, St Augustine, Thomas Aquinas and Jeanne Guyon. Many of the key artists of the West are discussed (many of them French): Charles Baudelaire, Stendhal, Georges Bataille, the troubadours, the *Romance of the Rose*, William Shakespeare, Dante Alighieri, André Gide, Paul Valéry, and Ovid. Kristeva applies her psychoanalysis to that perennial Freudian topic, love.

In *Histoires d'amour* Julia Kristeva brilliantly and lyrically combines psychoanalysis and poetry with a deep, sympathetic literary perception. Compared to so many dry, academic surveys of Western literature, which pour out of the universities and publishing houses by the dozen every year, Kristeva's *Tales of Love* is startlingly illuminating. To be treasured are her readings of Baudelaire's poetry, for example, or the troubadours. Kristeva knows what she's after, and doesn't waste time getting to it, unlike many other commentators. And if Kristeva does waffle (which is seldom), her meanderings are more worthy than most other critics' very best analyzes. Even when Kristeva doesn't appear to be saying much, she is saying more than most critics in their most concentrated passages.

For Julia Kristeva, love embodies both the semiotic and the symbolic, both knowledge and joy (*pace* Baruch de Spinoza), both language and affect (L, 170). Kristeva has written of love in a way that is not facile, demeaning, banal, stereotypical, sexist or pornographic. Her pronouncements on love are quite different from those in the 'classic' texts of love, such as Ovid's poems, or the mediæval *Art of Love*, or Elizabethan sonnet sequences, or Stendhal's *De l'Amour*, or Denis de Rougement's *L'Amour et l'occident* (*Love In the Western World*). When Kristeva writes –

> Vertigo of identity, vertigo of words: love, of the individual, is that sudden revelation, that irremediable cataclysm, of which one speaks only *after the fact*. Under its sway, one does not speak *of*. ("In Praise of Love", in TL, 3)

– it seems right and thankfully free of the usual embarrassment of sexism that marks most writing about love. Julia Kristeva evokes the wildness of love, the loss of self and the eruption of desire, without sounding idiotic. When Kristeva writes that in love one assumes one's right to be extraordinary, it is a great description of being in love. How right Kristeva is to describe love as the inrush of total subjectivity, an infinity of subjectivity. In Kristeva's psycho-poetic reading, love's the flood of the totally extraordinary, but at the expense of commonsense (as lovers learn, painfully):

> Love is the time and space in which "I" assumes the right to be extraordinary. Sovereign yet not individual. Divisible, lost, annihilated; but also, and through imaginary fusion with the loved one, equal to the infinite space of superhuman psychism. Paranoid? I am, in love, at the zenith of subjectivity. (TL, 5)

How great this first chapter of *Histoires d'amour* is, as great as Stendhal's *De l'Amour* or Sigmund Freud's *The Ego and the Id*, or Jacques Lacan's *Écrits*. Julia Kristeva describes love as a transgressive, sometimes violent wildness (D.H. Lawrence's term 'infinite sensual violence' is apposite here). 'Vertigo of identity, vertigo of words' – what a good turn of phrase. Vertigo – the falling in love, the fear of falling, the helplessness, the swoon into the abyss. Going over the edge. Moving beyond the boundaries. *Transgression.*

When Julia Kristeva writes in "In Praise of Love" about the pain of love, it is free of the usual sadomasochistic over/ undertones of the Marquis de Sade, Charles Baudelaire, Georges Bataille and André Breton. The pain of love, as Kristeva knows, underlines the miraculous nature of the experience of being in love – 'the experience of having been able to exist for, through, with another in mind' (TL, 4). This is Kristeva at her most idealistic, opened-out, her most overtly, self-consciously lyrical. Listen:

> As a bonus of desire, on the far and near side of pleasure, love skirts or displaces both in order to expand me to the dimensions of the universe.

Wow. Big stuff. An individual expanded to the size of the cosmos – the metaphor rules supreme! Julia Kristeva is certainly expansive and pellucid here. She continues (with some of my additions):

Expectancy [*the agony of anticipation*] makes me painfully sensitive [*lovers are always 'sensitive' souls*] to my incompleteness [*the 'without you I am nothing' cliché lovers gasp*], of which I was not aware *before* [*the identity crisis of love*]. For nor, while waiting [*there are endless hours waiting in love*], "before" and "after" become merged into a fearsome "never" [*lovers swear on eternities: 'stay with me 'til the End of Time!'*]. Love and the loved one erase the reckoning of time [*love as mystical timelessness*]... The *call*, its call, overwhelms me [*total subjectivity*] with a flow [*the old love as a flood metaphor*] in which the upheavals of the body [*love's sensuality/ biology*] (what people call emotions) are mingled with a whirling thought [*love as the fire bird which 'whirls' down an avenue of blues and yellows in Robert Graves's poem 'The Black Goddess'*], as vague, supple, ready to pierce [*love as sex*] or to wed [*love as marriage*] the other's as it is vigilant, alert, lucid in its impetus [*love as lucid (waking) dreaming, a cleansing of the doors of perception*]...towards what? Toward a destiny as relentless and blind as biological programming [*love as genetic force*], as the course of the species [*love as Darwinian survival*]... (TL, 5-6)

Julia Kristeva is speaking of love in the general sense, as it affects masses of people. What she says of love, though, has the ring of 'authentic' experience. None of this biographical take counts, though. What counts is:

A body swept away [this sentence continues from the above extract], present in all its limbs through a delightful absence – shaky voice, dry throat, starry eyes, flushed or clammy skin, throbbing heart... Would the symptoms of love be the symptoms of fear? Both a fear and a need of no longer being limited, held back, but going beyond. Dread of transgressing not only proprieties or taboos, but also, and above all, fear of crossing and desiring to cross the boundaries of the self... The *meeting*, then, mixing pleasure and promise or hopes, remains in a sort of future perfect. It is the nontime of love that, both instant and eternity, past and future, abreacted present, fulfils me, abolishes me, and yet leaves me unsated... Till tomorrow, forever, as ever, faithfully, eternally as before, as when it will have been, yours... (TL, 6)

What Julia Kristeva has produced with *Tales of Love* is a poet's or artist's handbook, a source book of the energies and drives that lie behind artistic creation. Basically, Kristeva's exploration of the origins of the artistic undertaking derives much from Sigmund Freud yet is not tainted by morbidity or an insistent reduction to sexual drives ('[r]eality is sex: that is Freud's starting point' [TL, 8]).[1] In Kristeva's poetics, sexuality is not all-consuming, as it is in Freud's work. While reading Freud's writing can be exhilarating, there is often a nagging sadness that stems from the perception of Freud's belief that so much of the richness of life can be reduced to one or two impulses. Is this all we are? This or that impulse? Maybe I've read Freud wrongly. Maybe it's impossible to read Freud 'purely' without being influenced by the vast amount of information, films, critical opinions, deconstructions, articles, and so on, that have collected around the man whose name means 'joy'.

Julia Kristeva's opening chapter of *Tales of Love* begins with Sigmund Freud's project, in particular his linking of love with narcissism. In a sense, at first glance, Kristeva appears to be more bleak in her outlook than even the arch-reductionist himself. After all, Kristeva insists on abjection, on a fundamental emptiness at the heart of the individual, on horror and suffering. Like Freud, Kristeva insists on the 'madness' of love, on seeing love as a form of madness. She notes that Freud made this observation especially caustic. Thanks to Freud, it's known that it is not so much the object of love that is really important as love itself, as it is experienced by the individual. Objects are one thing, but without the individual experiencing love at first hand, everything that follows is rendered void.

Julia Kristeva's "Freud and Love" lucidly opens up the relationships between the individual and love, between identification and narcissism, between the 'madness' of love and the libido. What emerges in Kristeva's psychoanalytical view of love is a mode of going to extremes founded on primal, archaic identifications and instincts. 'All desire is connected to madness', Luce Irigaray asserted in *Sexes et parentés* (I, 35).

Love, in the philosophies of Sigmund Freud and Julia Kristeva, is not something calmly dissected by scientists on an operating table in the controlled conditions of the laboratory, but a blindness and madness experienced by people regressing swift as an arrow to the primal, libidinal stages of psycho-sexual growth.

Love, for Julia Kristeva, following the Freudian model, is a means of identification and abdication:

> Amatory identification, *Einfühlung* (the assimilation of other people's feelings), appears to be madness when seen in the light of Freud's caustic lucidity: the ferment of collective hysteria in which crowds abdicate their own judgment, a hypnosis that causes us to lose percept- ion of reality since we hand it over in the *Ego Ideal*. The object in hyp- nosis devours or absorbs the ego, the voice of consciousness becomes blurred, "in loving blindness one becomes a criminal without remorse" – *the object has taken the place of what was the ego ideal*. (*Tales of Love*, 24- 25)

The relation between love and language for Julia Kristeva pivots around primary narcissism:

> ...when one transposes into language the idealization on the edge of primal repression that amatory experience amounts to, this assumes that scription and writer invest in language in the first place precisely because it is a favourite object – a place for excess and absurdity, and ecstasy and death. Putting love into words... necessarily summons up not the narcissistic *parry* but what appears to me as narcissistic *economy*. (TL, 267-8)

Writing of love perpetuates the 'narcissistic economy'. To explore her psychoanalytic theory of love, Julia Kristeva often employs the tactic of setting things against each other, of opposites. Thus, she explores the realm of the obverse of love – hate. In her essay on *Romeo and Juliet*, Kristeva writes:

> If desire is fickle, thirsting for novelty, unstable by definition, what is it that leads love to dream of an eternal couple? Why faithfulness, the wish for a durable harmony, why in short a marriage of love – not as necessity in a given society but as desire, as libidinal necessity? ("Romeo and Juliet: Love-Hatred in the Couple", in TL, 225)

The problem is that love and the couple is always problematized, is always fraught with problems. Maybe it's because, as Sigmund Freud suggests, in the narcissism of love, hatred is deeper and more ancient than love. Thus, adultery becomes more correctly termed betrayal – of the deepest parts of the self, a betrayal of identity and narcissism. Interestingly, in her discussion of *Romeo and Juliet*, Kristeva suggests that death maybe an essential ingredient in romantic love: that is, without death, love itself dies (by turning to hate). 'Death, therefore, becomes the protection against the normal, banal couple in marriage', wrote John Lechte (L, 176).

Where this widespread dream of a total and eternal love between adults comes from is a highly complex question, not solvable by observing people only in a Freudian fashion, nor by looking at cultural influences, nor by economic factors alone. Somehow, being together in a sexual, romantic relationship is deemed essential in First World, Western, bourgeois countries. Heterosexuality, as Adrienne Rich suggested, is 'compulsory', just as one is expected to be sexual too, whatever one's sexual orientation. Sex; one must be having it, or, if not, one *must* be wanting it. Those who step outside of the Heterosexual Togetherness Law are alienated. The desire for the other is consuming, but, as Kristeva and thousands of others have noted, it brings with it immense problems, some of them insurmountable. (Simone de Beauvoir noted that 'marriage is dangerous for a woman' (M, 147), because she loses part of her independence and identity). Kristeva's comments upon serial monogamy, to which people seem to be committed in the West, are illuminating. For, although the desire for the other drives people onward, it also upsets their psychic equilibrium:

> As soon as an *other* appears different from myself, it becomes alien, repelled, repugnant, abject – hated. (TL, 22, also 1982)

Part of the problem of love, as Sigmund Freud knew well (but so did love poets like William Shakespeare, Dante Alighieri and Sappho) is that the lover turns the beloved into an object. 'The lover is a narcissist with an *object*', remarks Julia Kristeva (TL, 33).

In Plato's *Symposium*, love is of/ for the other, the other half of one's being. One searches for the completeness to be found in the beloved. The beloved thus becomes that missing fragment which rounds out the desiring self. In Neoplatonism (which followed and developed Plato's thought), there is a shift towards a different kind of narcissism. In Plotinus' *Enneads*, love is God, but God is also Narcissus. In Plotinus, the One is 'simultaneously the *loved one* and *love*; He is *love of himself*; for He is beautiful only by and in Himself' (*Enneads*, VI, 8, 15). With Neoplatonism, a new kind of love is born, one founded on interiority and autoeroticism. Narcissus loves himself, he is both subject and object. His real object of desire is an image of himself – that is, representation, art. Kristeva writes in "Narcissus: The New Insanity":

> He loves, he loves Himself – active and passive, subject and object... *The object of Narcissus is psychic space; it is representation itself, fantasy.* But he does not know it, and he dies. If he knew it he would be an intellectual, a creator of speculative fictions, an artist, writer, psychologist, psychoanalyst. He would be Plotinus or Freud. (In TL, 116)

Narcissus in Ovid's poem is in love with an image, a representation of the beloved (himself), much as the artist is. Although he kills himself for falling in love with a fake, Narcissus nevertheless goes about dealing with his idealism by fetishizing his own image. As Julia Kristeva remarks, 'instead of having to *create* what will enable him to equal his ideal – a work, or an idealized object to love – Narcissus will *fabricate* an *ersatz*' (ib., 126). This is what lovers in literature do. They create the idealism from their projections. Poets are in love with their self-created images. They have to be: it's their 'truth'. Poets are 'fascinated by images on the one hand, in quest of truth on the other' (ib., 131). Artists recognize their love of images even as they adore them. The two things, representation and 'reality', constantly fuse in a way that still confuses observers. Non-artists still get confused about the relation between illusion and the 'real' world (think of the confusions that arise when people think of 'Shakespeare Country' in the Bard's plays, and conflate it with Stratford, Warwickshire and London in England).

✤

JULIA KRISTEVA

Julia Kristeva inevitably approaches the *Song of Songs*, that ecstatic and very erotic poem sequence which sits so oddly in the rest of the *Old Testament*. In the *Songs of Songs* Kristeva sees again the deep-seated links between art and love, between love imagined and love 'real'. The *Song of Songs* is, as Kristeva says in her excellent analysis of it ("A Holy Madness: She and He", in *Tales of Love*), significant because it allows the female Shulamite lover as much expression as the male. 'The amorous dialogue is tension and *jouissance*, repetition and infinity; not as communication but as *incantation*. Song dialogue. *Invocation'*, Kristeva writes (1987, 93). It's clear to Kristeva that the psychic or inner space of the *Song of Songs* is inseparable from the amorous space. Or vice versa, more accurately. What appears to be 'realistic' gestures and emotions are all manufactured and theatrical. Erotic desire energizes and drives the poem sequence, but it's art – that is, the imagination – that shapes and finishes the project. Kristeva wrote in "A Holy Madness: She and He":

> As intersection of corporeal passion and idealization, love is undisputably the privileged experience for the blossoming of metaphor (abstract for concrete, concrete for abstract) as well as incarnation (the spirit becoming flesh, the word-flesh). Unless incarnation is a metaphor that has slipped into the real and has been taken for reality? A hallucination that is assumed to be real on account of the violence of amorous passion, which is in fact the ordinary manifestation of an alienation that confuses the fields of representation (real – imaginary – symbolic?)
> (TL, 95)

Again, one thinks not only of the *Song of Songs*, to which Julia Kristeva is referring here, but also the history of love poetry from Ovid through Francesco Petrarch to Emily Dickinson. For Kristeva, the *Song of Songs* is fascinating because of 'its being a legitimation of the impossible, an impossibility set up as amatory law' (ib., 97). Kristeva rightly recognizes in the Shulamite of the *Song of Songs* one of the first appearances of a sovereign woman, someone who is the equal of her lover, who is 'limpid, intense, divided, quick, upright, suffering, hoping' (TL, 100).

❧

As Julia Kristeva works her way in *Tales of Love* through the many forms of love depicted in Western culture, from Plato to William Shakespeare and beyond, what becomes more and more important is the text, rather than love – art, rather than desire. By the time Kristeva reaches the God of British literature, the Bard, it is clear that the interweaving of text and love is inextricable. Treating characters as 'real' humans rather than paper figments becomes more and more problematic.

Julia Kristeva's observations on William Shakespeare ring true for many melodramas of love. For example, she notes that Shakespeare's lovers in *Romeo and Juliet* spend more time getting ready to die than loving. This death-wish is at heart of Western depictions of love. In Francesco Petrarch's *Canzoniere*, the poet spends much more time whingeing about love than loving. He dwells obsessively on the death of his beloved Laura. As if, in dying, she attains mythic status. Similarly, Shakespeare's young lovers dwell manically on their obsessive, accursed affair (TL, 210). The *performance* of their love, played out against the warring families, against their peers, against the socio-political world of the play, becomes more significant than their love itself. The experience is not enough. There must be performance and dialogue. Love becomes a discourse. Metaphor takes over.

One of the more intriguing insights into William Shakespeare's writing is when Julia Kristeva wonders what would have happened if Shakespeare's lovers, Romeo and Juliet, had survived. They would not, she says in "Romeo And Juliet: Love-Hatred in the Couple", become like Antony and Cleopatra, or the aged lovers in *A Winter's Tale*:

> Either time's alchemy transforms the criminal, secret passion of the outlaw lovers into the banal, humdrum, lacklustre lassitude of a tired and cynical collusion: that is the normal marriage. Or else the married couple continues to be a passionate couple, but covering the entire gamut of sadomasochism that the two partners heralded in the yet relatively quiet version of the Shakespearean text. Each acting out both sexes in turn they thus create a foursome that feeds on itself through repeated aggression and merging, castration and gratification, resurrection and death. (TL, 217)

Then Julia Kristeva comes to the many functions of art, one of which is, for the artist, to prolong and recapture and rework that which no longer exists. If you can't love, then write your way out of your predicament. If the imaginary is 'real', then virtual loving is the same as 'real' loving. Love exists in a nostalgic past or in a never-to-be-attained future. 'The *meeting*, then, mixing pleasure and promise or hopes, remains in a sort of future perfect', comments Kristeva ("In Praise of Love" [in TL, 6]). The only way to deal with the impossibility of love in writing, it seems, is to enter the empire of the metaphor. 'The language of love is impossible, inadequate, immediately allusive when one would like it to be most straightforward; it is a flight of metaphors – it is literature', states Kristeva (TL, 1). She continues, on her 'philosophy of love': '[f]or what is psychoanalysis if not an infinite quest for rebirths through the experience of love...?' (ib.) If the poet has to jump into metaphor, so does the critic or psychoanalyst. They all trade in language. But talking about love, Kristeva admits, 'seems to me different from living it, but no less troublesome and delightfully intoxicating. Does this sound ridiculous? It is mad' (TL, 2).

Discussing Charles Baudelaire, Julia Kristeva says that in the 'incandescence of Romantic metaphoricalness', which is the poet's way of writing,

metaphor becomes antithetical, as if to blur all reference, and ends up as synæsthesia, as if to open up the Word to the passion of the body itself, as it is.[2]

Julia Kristeva writes in "Baudelaire, or Infinity, Perfume, and Punk":

Perfume is thus the most powerful metaphor for that archaic universe, preceding sight, where what takes place is the conveyance of the most opaque lovers' indefinite identities, together with the chilliest words: 'There are strong perfumes for all matter/ Is porous. They seem to penetrate glass.' (*Tales of Love*, 334)

For Julia Kristeva, in Charles Baudelaire's poetry perfume is the metaphor of condensation – Sigmund Freud's sense of love.

The poetic zone Arthur Rimbaud, Charles Baudelaire, Comte de Lautréamont, Friedrich Hölderlin and other poets speak of or strive for is similar to Julia Kristeva's notion of the dark, pre-œdipal space of the mother, the *chora*. Michael Payne defines Kristeva's *chora* thus: 'a nourishing and maternal, pre-verbal semiotic space or state in which the linguistic sign has not yet been articulated as the absence of an object' (239). Rimbaud's alchemy of the word is partly founded, like Kristeva's *chora*, on the maternal body as an actuality. As Kristeva writes in *Desire in Language*:

> Cells fuse, split, and proliferate; volumes grow, tissues stretch, and body fluids change rhythm, speeding up or slowing down. Within the body, growing as a graft, indomitable, there is an other. (237)

The 'other' is the child; the poet is pregnant with a different sort of child: her/ his art, the poem, the artwork as the Magical Child of alchemy. In *Revolution as Poetic Language*, Julia Kristeva speaks of the *chora* as the place where 'the subject is both generated and negated' (28); it is 'a place of change, it is fluid, amorphous, 'pre-word', and, like a cell, divisible' (ib., 239-240n.). Language, though, can never circumscribe this maternal space: to name it is to change it.

Julia Kristeva's notion of the semiotic modality and the *chora* links trenchantly with Arthur Rimbaud's poetic quest, especially if one considers Rimbaud's deeply ambiguous Oedipal feelings and his confused, anxious relationship with his mother.

Unable to be in love, the poet may then write of love and literally recreate love, make love anew. Writing of love unleashes 'a whole, imaginary, uncontrollable, undecidable flood' (TL, 3). Writing, Julia Kristeva suggests, may be 'synonymous with the amatory condition'.[3] Love poetry may prolong love by writing of love. This is a new *jouissance* of the text, where, in a synæsthetic blur, writing of love becomes equivalent to love itself. In "Joyce, le retour d'Orphée", Kristeva remarks that the amorous and artistic experiences as two interependent aspects of the identificatory process, are our only way of preserving our psychic space as a "living system", that is, open to the other, capable of adaption and change (5)

The poet might, in the process of writing, produce 'the very possibility of his *jouissance*'.4 Instead of always being 'after the fact', writing of love – especially in those realms of writing such as poetry which use tons of metaphors – may replicate or evoke love itself in a new *jouissance*, a *jouissance* of presence. Of course this is wild idealism. But why not? People live largely in imaginary worlds (culture) which are set within larger fictional constructs (society), which is inside another fiction (the universe). The last religion, says Julia Kristeva, is art: 'we are all the faithful of the last religion, the esthetic one. We are all subjects of the metaphor.'5

> In love with himself without knowing it, a victim of his sight that appears to him as creating the world, the poet tends to mistake the world for a show – arbitrary, false, liable to be manipulated by himself. Out of uprightness, however, he turns away from it and, to punish himself, closes his eyes. (TL, 132)

Discussing Georges Bataille's *My Mother*, Julia Kristeva makes remarks which apply to so much of post-Romantic art. Her analysis of modern sexual literature reckons that its project is to reproduce the 'flash' of the sublime, something like James Joyce's 'epiphany'. The erotic moves into meditation and expansion. Kristeva writes in "Bataille and the Sun, or the Guilty Text":

> Erotic fantasy merges with philosophical meditation in order to reach the focus where the sublime and the abject, making up the pedestal of love, come together in the "flash." …The contemporary narrative (from Joyce to Bataille) has a posttheological aim: to communicate the amorous flash. The one in which the "I" reaches the paranoid dimensions of the sublime divinity while remaining close to abject collapse, disgust with the self. Or, quite simply, to its moderate version known as solitude. (In TL, 368)

If art comes out of the 'crises of subjectivity' (1984, 131-2), as Julia Kristeva suggests, and any number of artists' work could be cited to support her theory, then melancholy and solitude are inevitable. Melancholy is indeed the natural state of many poets and writers – especially love poets (think of Francesco Petrarch, Bernard de Ventadour, Giraut de Borneil, Emily Brontë, Emily Dickinson, William Shakespeare, Louise Labé, and so on). Kristeva aligns this depressive poetic melancholy with the metaphoric expression of the repressed maternal element. Kristevan melancholy is aligned with the mother and death: melancholia derives in part from an unsuccessful separation from the mother (J. Lechte, 1990b, 34).

The artist writes of love to bring back love. Metaphor becomes the mechanisms by which love is reactivated, metaphor becomes 'the point at which ideal and affect come together in language', commented John Lechte.[6] Love and art are united through metaphor. Metaphor enables love to exist in poetry. So important is writing and making art for some artists, they feel they are not really 'alive' unless they are making art. Many is the writer who does not feel a day has been spent well unless it has involved some writing. Writers often speak of feeling uneasy (or guilty) if they have not been writing. Literature is full of characters who scribble scribble scribble. Writing not only enlarges life, it is central to the life of some writers. André Gide wrote copiously in his journal, while Henry Miller, John Cowper Powys and Rainer Maria Rilke were obsessive, prolific letter writers. For Gide, his life needed to be mythicized in literature.

> It is, very simply, through the work and the play of signs [commented Kristeva], a crisis of subjectivity which is the basis for all creation, one which takes as its every precondition the possibility of survival. I would even say that signs are what produce a body, that – and the artist knows it well – if he doesn't work, if he doesn't produce his music or his page or his sculpture, he would be, quite simply, ill or not alive. (1984, 131-2)

For Julia Kristeva, lovers, like artists, create from a feeling of lack, loss or pain. The lover, like the artist, is a wounded creature in Kristeva's reading. Both the lover and artist are 'reality fools', to use Lawrence Durrell's term. They are mistaken about their interpretation of reality. Kristeva says that:

> The speaking being is a wounded being, his speech wells up out of an aching for love... ("Extraterrestrials Suffering For Want of Love", TL, 372)

Artists know, though, that their many-faceted, ambiguous and sometimes glorious creations do not compensate for the wound. Art never has done, and never will. But maybe knowing a little about the wound, and contemplating what thinkers such as Julia Kristeva have said about the wound, helps a little.

Of the thousands of thinkers who've written about art and artistic creation, the works of Julia Kristeva are undoubtedly some of the most illuminating and thought-provoking in the contemporary cultural arena. But Kristeva is such an inspiring philosopher, that her views on art and artists are only a fraction of her overall output, which takes in so many areas of experience and culture and society.

By any standards, Julia Kristeva is an extraordinary writer.

✤

ILLUSTRATIONS

Images of Julia Kristeva.

Images of some of the people who have influenced her,
and people that she has studied.
Also, some painting by Giovanni Bellini.

On this page and the following pages
are some artists and thinkers discussed
by Julia Kristeva, or associated with her work.

Friedrich Nietzsche (below).

Friedrich Hölderlin

Novalis

Arthur Rimbaud

Antonin Artaud, above.
Georges Bataille, below.

Sigmund Freud

Jacques Derrida, above.
Jacques Lacan, below.

Luce Irigaray

Hélène Cixous

Monique WItttig

Giovanni Bellini, Virgin and Child, Metropolitan Museum,
New York City

Giovanni Bellini, The Virgin and Child, Pinacoteca de Brera, Milan

Giovanni Bellini, Virgin and Child, Museo Correr, Venice

Giovanni Bellini, Madonna of the Meadow,
National Gallery, London

Giovanni Bellini, The Virgin and Child, Bergamo

Giovanni Bellini, Madonna and Child Enthroned, 1488, Venice

Giovanni Bellini, The Coronation of the Virgin, Pesaro

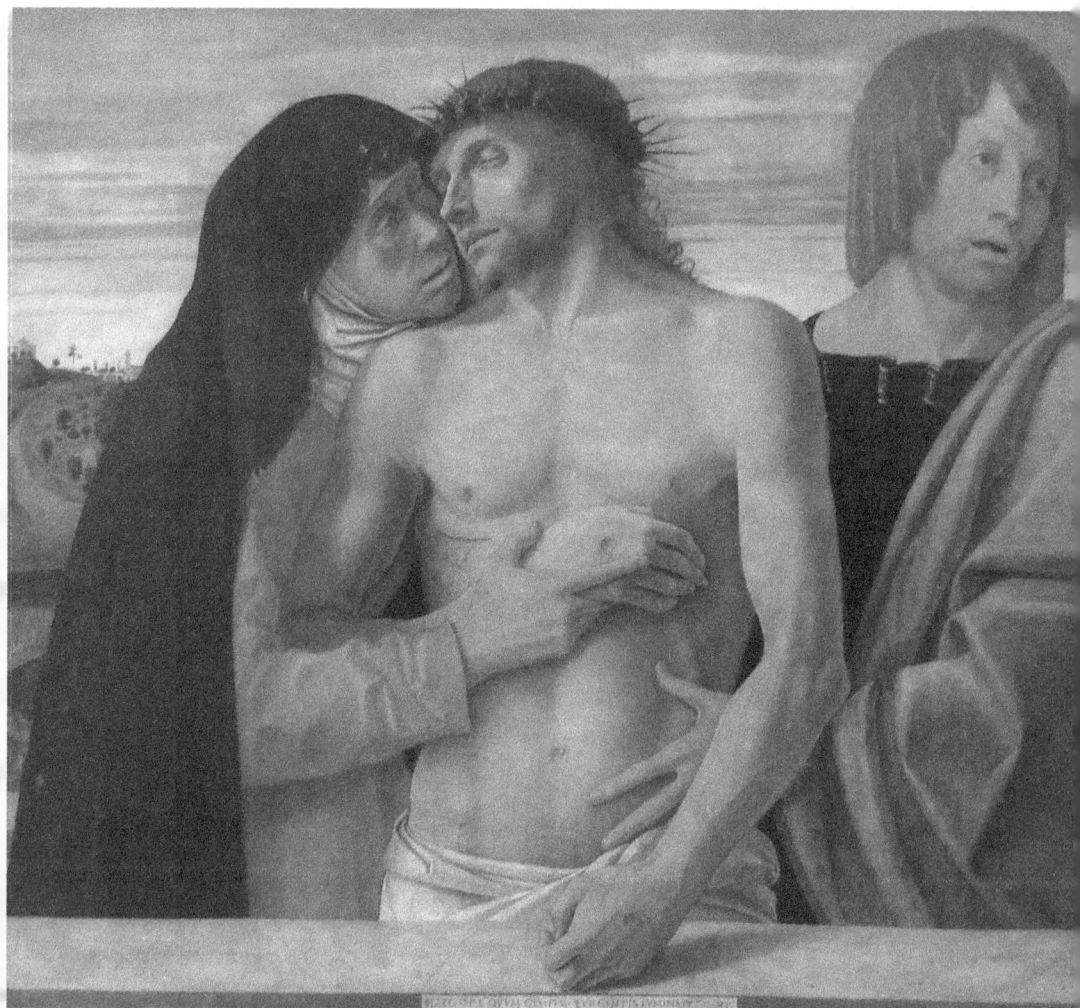

Giovanni Bellini, Pietà, Milan

NOTES

PREFACE

1. S. Jackson: "Gender and Heterosexuality: A Materialist Feminist Analysis", in M. Maynard, 1994, 13.
2. S. Jackson, op.cit., 1995.
3. See Gayatri Chakravorty Spivak, 1981.
4. A. Huyssen, "Mapping the postmodern", *New German Critique*, 33, 1984, 16.

1. INTRODUCTORY

1. Katherine Stephenson, in E. Sartori, 230.
2. R. Barthes: "L'Etrangère", *La Quinzaine littéraire*, May, 1970, 19.
3. Julia Kristeva has written lucidly, for example, of her 'mother tongue'. John Lechte writes:

She is hypersensitive to the maternal, the familiar, and the same. Such may well be the source of her legendary 'difficulty': what she is talking about is so close to us that it becomes difficult to grasp intellectually. (1990a, 81)

4. Marxist-Feminist Literature Collective: "Women's Writing", *Ideology and Consciousness*, 1, 3, Spring, 1978, 30.

2. FRENCH FEMINIST POETICS

1. "A partir de *Polylogue*", 1977, 495f.
2. H. Cixous: "Castration or Decapitation?", *Signs*, 7, 1, 52.
3. See Arleen B. Dallery; Deborah Cameron; Jan Montefiore; Andrea Nye, 1989.
4. M. Wittig: "The Straight Mind", *Feminist Issues*, 1, 1, 110.
5. Luce Irigaray: *Parler n'est jamais neutre*, tr. David Macey, in I, 94.
6. 'When poetry becomes a hypostatization of semiotic motility, it can also be seen as a refusal of the thetic' (M. Payne, 175), but Kristeva does not advocate that the thetic is rejected. Of society, Kristeva says that 'subjects are called upon to participate in a law whose determinations and articulations they neither know nor control' (RL, 478).
7. Mary Ellman: *Thinking About Women*, Harcourt, New York, 1968, 6.
8. Marxist-Feminist Literature Collective: "Women's Writing: *Jane Eyre, Shirley, Villette, Aurora Leigh*", in Francis Barker *et al*, eds. *1848: The Sociology of Literature*, in M. Eagleton, 1986, 197.
9. Mary Ann Doane is sceptical: this seemingly desirable place of the French feminists is in fact a 'nonplace' (1988).
10. See, for example, Kelly Oliver: "Who is Nietzsche's Woman?", in B. On, 1994, and "Nietzsche's 'Woman'", *Radical Philosophy*, 48, 1988; Jean Graybeal: *Language and "the Feminine" in Nietzsche and Heidegger*, Indiana University Press, Bloomington, 1990; D. Krell, 1986; D. O'Hara, 1985; Sarah Kofman: *Nietzsche et la scéne philosophique*, Union générale d'éditions, Paris, 1979; S. Kofman: "Baubô", in M. Gillespie; Carol Diethe: "Nietzsche and the Woman Question", *History of European Ideas*, 11, 1989; Gary Schapiro: *Alcyone: Nietzsche on Gifts, Noise, and Women*, SUNY, Albany, 1991; O. Schutte: "Nietzsche on Gender Difference", in B. On; Michael Platt: "Woman, Nietzsche, and Nature", *Maieutis*, 2, 1981; Gayle L. Ormiston: "Traces of Derrida: Nietzsche's Image of Woman", *Philosophy Today*, 28, 1984; L. Baker, 1989; E. Behler, 1988.
11. J. Derrida, *Spurs*, 101; see also D. Krell, 1986.
12. See Kelly Oliver; Sarah Kofman, op. cit.
13. F. Nietzsche: *Briefe an Peter Gast*, Leipzig, 1924, 89-90.
14. Janet Lungstrum: "Nietzsche Writing Woman/ Woman Writing Nietzsche", in P. Burgard, 144.

15. Sarah Kofman: *L'Enigma de la femme: La femme dans les textes de Freud*, Galilée, Paris, 1980. See also Biddy Martin: *Woman and Modernity: The (Life)Styles of Lou Andreas-Salomé*, Cornell University Press, Ithaca 1991.

16. L. Andreas-Salomé: "Die in sich ruhende Frau", in *Zur Psychologie der Frau*, ed. Giselda Brinker-Gabler, Fischer, Frankfurt, 1978, 295-6.

17. Both Arkady Plotinsky and Alan D. Schrift use Hélène Cixous' ecstatic text "The Laugh of the Medusa", and "Sorties" (A. Plotinsky: "The Medusa's Ears: The Question of Nietzsche, the Question of Gender, and Transformation of Theory", A. Schrift: "On the Gynecology of Morals: Nietzsche and Cixous on the Logic of the Gift", both in P. Burgard).

18. See John Lechte: "Art, Love, and Melancholy in the Work of Julia Kristeva", in J. Fletcher, 39.

19. Kelly Oliver: "Nietzsche's Abjection", in P. Burgard, 60.

20. F. Nietzsche: *The Birth of Tragedy*, tr. W. Kaufmann, Vintage, New York, 1967, §16, p. 104; F. Nietzsche: *Ecce Homo*, in *On the Genealogy of Morals* and *Ecce Homo*, Vintage, New York, 1967, 266.

21. See P. Burgard, 235; see also S. Kofman, Schirft, J. Lungstrum, *et al*, in the same volume; also, H. Cixous' "Sorties" and *Newly-Born Woman*.

22. Luce Irigaray: *Speculum of the Other Woman*, tr. Gillian C. Gill, and *This Sex Which Is Not One*, tr. Catherine Porter, both Cornell University Press, New York, 1985; see also: Dorothy Leland: "Lacanian psychoanalysis and French feminism: toward an adequate political psychology", *Hypatia*, 3, 3, Winter, 1989, 81-103.

23. Elizabeth Grosz: "Refiguring Lesbian Desire", in L. Doan, 75.

24. R.M. Rilke, letter to Clara Rilke, 8 March, 1907, in *Gesammalte Briefe 1892-1926*, Insel Verlag, Leipzig, 1940, II, 279f.

25. Maggie Humm: "Is the gaze feminist? Pornography, film and feminism", *Perspectives on Pornography*, eds. G. Day & C. Bloom, Macmillan, 1988; L. Gamman, 1988; E.D. Pribram, 1988.

26. J. Lacan, "The meaning of the phallus", 1988; Bernard Baas: "Le désir pur", *Ornicar?*, 83, 1987; R. Lapsley, 1992.

27. C. Jung: *The Development of Personality*, vol. 17, Routledge, 1954, 198; Marie-Louise von Franz: *The Psychological Meaning of Redemption Motifs in Fairy Tales*, Inner City Books, Toronto, 1980, 39f.

28. Emma Jung & Marie-Louise von Franz: *The Grail Legend*, tr. Andrea Dykes, Sigo Press, Boston, Mass., 1980, 64.

29. Hélène Cixous writes: '[m]en say that there are two unrepresentable things: death and the feminine sex. That's because they need femininity to be associated with death; it's the jitters that give them a hard-on! For themselves! They need to be afraid of us' ("The Laugh of

the Medusa", M, 255).

30. Larysa Mykyta: "Lacan, Literature and the Look", *SubStance*, 39, 1983, 54.
31. See Laura Mulvey: "Visual pleasure and narrative cinema", *Screen*, vol. 16, no. 3, 1975, 6-19.
32. Catherine King: "The Politics of Representation: A Democracy of the Gaze", in F. Bonner, 136.
33. Luce Irigaray, "Women's Exile", in D. Cameron, 1990, 83; and Luce Irigaray: *Speculum*.
34. Emma Pérez: "Irigaray's Female Symbolic in the Making of Chicana Lesbian *Sitios y Lenguas* (*Sites and Discourses*)", in L. Doan, 108.

3. FRENCH FEMINISM, SEXUALITY, AND SEXUAL DIFFERENCE

1. Xavière Gauthier, in M, 201-2.
2. L. Irigaray: "Ce sexe qui n'en est pas un", M, 103; see also: Jane Gallop, 1983, 77-83; Elizabeth Grosz: "Philosophy, subjectivity and the body", in C. Pateman, 1986, 125-43.
3. Moira Gatens: "Power, Bodies and Difference", in M. Barrett, 1992, 134.
4. A. Jones: "Writing the Body", in E. Showalter, 1986, 369.
5. Audre Lorde: *Sister Outsider*, Crossing Press, New York, 1984, and in M. Humm, 1992, 283.
6. Sue Miller: *The Good Mother*, Harper & Row, New York, 1986.
7. Summer Brenner: *The Soft Room*, Figures, 1978.
8. Susan Griffin: *Viyella*, in Laura Chester, 326.
9. See, for instance, Lonnie Barbach, ed. *Pleasures: Women Write Erotica*, Doubleday, New York, 1984; Laura Duesing: *Three West Coast Women*, Five Fingers Poetry, 1987; Clayton Eshleman, ed. *Caterpillar Anthology*, Anchor, 1971; Lynne Tillman: *Weird Fucks*, 1980; Jane Hirshfield: *Of Gravity and Angels*, Wesleyan University Press, 1988; Jayne Anne Phillips: *Black Tickets*, Delacorte Press, 1979; Marilyn Hacker: *Love, Death and the Changing of the Seasons*, Arbor House, 1986; Nancy Friday: *Forbidden Flowers: More Women's Sexual Fantasies*, Arrow, 1993.
10. Xavière Gauthier, in M, 201-2.
11. Catherine MaKinnon: "Feminism, Marxism, Method, and the State: An Agenda for Theory", in N.O. Keohane, ed. *Feminist Theory: A Critique of Ideology*, Harvester, 1982.
12. Elaine Marks, "Lesbian Intertextuality", in G. Stambolian, 376.
13. Marilyn Farewell: "Toward Definition of the Lesbian Literary

Imagination", *Signs*, 14, 1988, 98.

14. Namascar Shaktini: "Displacing the Phallic Subject: Wittig's Lesbian Writing", *Signs*, 8, 1, Autumn, 1982, 29.

15. Dianne Chisholm, "Lesbianism", in E. Wright, 1992, 217.

16. See Marina Warner: *Monuments and Maidens*, Weidenfeld & Nicholson, 1985; Kenneth Clark: *The Nude*, Pantheon Books, 1957; Lynda Nead, 19.

17. Sherry B. Ortner, 1982.

18. Edwin Ardener: "Belief and the Problem of Women", in Shirley Ardener, ed. *Perceiving Women*, Halsted Press, New York, 1978.

19. Myra Jehlen: "Archimedes and the paradox of feminist criticism", *Signs*, 6, 4, 1981, 575f.

20. Elaine Showalter: "Feminist Criticism in the Wilderness", in E. Showalter, 1986, 262-3; J. Roberts, 1991, 1-5.

21. Sherry B. Ortner, 1982.

22. Ann Rosalind Jones: "Writing the Body: L'Écriture féminine", in E. Showalter, 1986, 363.

23. A. Jardine, "Opaque Texts", in N. Miller, 1986, 109.

24. Victor Burgin: "Geometry and Abjection", in J. Fletcher, 115-6.

25. Luce Irigaray: "La différence sexuelle", *Ethiope de la différence sexuelle*, Minuit, Paris, 1984, and in Toril Moi, 1988, 128.

26. J. Kristeva: "La femme, ce n'est jamais ça", *Tel Quel*, Autumn, 1974, in M, 135.

27. M. Duras, interview in *Signs*, Winter, 1975, in M, 175.

28. C. Burke, 1981, 289; J. Sayers, 1982, 132; C. Faure, 1981, 85.

29. See Susan Rubin Suleiman: "(Re)Writing the Body: The Politics of Female Eroticism", in S. Suleiman, 14f; Elizabeth Grosz, 1988, 28-33; Alison M. Jaggar, 1989; Naomi Schor, 1989, 38-58.
    For Griselda Pollock, Julia Kristeva's emphasis in her æsthetics of painting on the 'feminine' encourages seeing 'woman as difference, inchoate, unspeakable, enigmatic, metaphor for all that is outside representation and meaning except as lack' ("Painting, Feminism, History", in M. Barrett, 1992, 157).

30. Monique Witting: "One Is Not Born a Woman", speech at the Feminist as Scholar Conference, May, 1979, Barnard College, New York.

31. E. Showalter: "Feminist Criticism in the Wilderness", in E. Showalter, 1986, 250.

32. French feminists, such as Hélène Cixous and Luce Irigaray, do not claim to 'represent' *all* women or 'women' as a concept (M. Gatens, in M. Barrett, 1992, 134).

33. See also J. Sayers, 1986, 42; T. Moi, 1985, 110; H. Wenzel, 1981, 284; M. Plaza, 1978.

34. R. DuPlessis, 1985, 273; S. Gilbert, 1986, xvi; M. Hite, 1988, 123.

4. JULIA KRISTEVA'S QUEST

1. Julia Kristeva: "Jackson Pollock's Milky Way, 1912-56", 34-39.
2. Andreas Huyssen: *After the Great Divide: Modernism, Mass Culture and Postmodernism*, Macmillan, 1986, 55f.
3. T. Moi, in K, 13; J. Féral, 1978, 8; A. Nye, 1987, 673; A. Jardine, 1985, 228.
4. Another (more politically barbed) version of the shaman or outsider is the intellectual dissident, which Julia Kristeva discussed in an essay that appeared in *Tel Quel* ("Un nouveau type d'intellectuel: le dissident", 1977). S.R. Suleiman says 'I feel much drawn to [Kristeva's] evocation of the 'happy cosmopolitan', foreign not only to others but to him- or herself, harboring not an absence but a 'pulverized origin'' (S. Suleiman, 1990, 25).
5. Peter Redgrove: *The Laborators*, Taxus, 1993, 10.
6. Jennifer Stone: "The horror of power: A critique of 'Kristeva'", in F. Barker, 1983, 38-48.
7. Michel Foucault: *The Order of Things*, Tavistock, 1970; Fredric Jameson: "Postmodernism or the Cultural Logic of Late Capitalism", in *Postmodernism, or the Cultural Logic of Late Capitalism*, Verso, London, 1991.
8. Jean Baudrillard: *America*, Verso, 1988.
9. Rosi Braidotti: *Patterns of Dissonance*, Polity Press, 1991, 14.
10. Jacques Derrida: *Psyché: inventions de l'autre*, Galilée, 1987, 562.
11. Martin Heidegger: *Der Satz vom Grund*, Pfullingen, Neske, 1957.
12. Martin Heidegger: *What is Called Thinking?*, Harper & Row, New York, 1968.
13. Martin Heidegger: *Nietzsche*, vol. 2, Harper & Row, New York, 1984; David Levin: *The Body's Recollection of Being: Phenomenological Psychology and the Deconstruction of Nihilism*, Routledge, 1985.
14. Jacques Derrida: "Chora", *Poikilia: études offertes à Jean-Pierre Vernant*, Éditions de l'École des Hautes Études en Sciences Sociales, Paris 1987.

5. THE PSYCHOLOGY OF THE ARTIST IN JULIA KRISTEVA'S PHILOSOPHY

1. Julia Kristeva's *chora* is 'on the borderline between all polarities:

between being and nothing, idealism and materialism, sacred and profane, silence and language', Philippa Berry remarked ("Woman and space according to Kristeva and Irigaray", in P. Berry, 256).

2. Kate Chedgzoy: "Frida Kahlo's 'grotesque' bodies", in P. Florence, 1995, 45.

3. Julia Kristeva writes in "Postmodernism?" of the *avant garde* modernists' writing as an

exploration of the typical imaginary relationship, that of the mother, through the most radical and problematic aspect of this relationship, language. This relationship returns to the presymbolic, to an arrangement of rhythms and alliterations that either stands up against meaning or shapes it. (in P. Brooker, 201).

4. John Lechte glosses the relation of Julia Kristevan semiotics to poetic creation thus:

When Kristeva says that 'no language can sing unless it confronts the Phallic Mother' [DL, 191], she means that no progress can be made in the presentation of genitality (difference) in the text unless the negativity-rejection of 'music in letters' pluralizes the imaginary, mystical unity of a mother at the origins of the symbolic who, *qua* unity, becomes masculinzed. And so because the musicalization of language is bound up with the individual's relation to others, sexuality is fundamental to textuality' (J. Lechte, 1990a, 152-3).

6. JULIA KRISTEVA AND PAINTING

1. For Julia Kristeva, the Virgin Mary was a compromise solution to the problem of women's paranoia; the Virgin Mary was a sublimation of the woman's murderous desires through the valorization of her breast, and the pain, a fantasy of eternity (in the *Assumption*), a denial of other women, including the Virgin's own mother, a denial of men's part in procreation (the virgin birth). Susan Suleiman writes:

the mother, according to Kristeva, the Other is not (only) an arbitrary sign, a necessary absence; it is the child, whose presence and whose bodily link to her are inescapable givens, material facts. If to love (her child) is, for a woman, the same thing as to write, we have in that conjunction a modern secular equivalent of the word made flesh. (1995, 27)

7. JULIA KRISTEVA'S THEORY OF LOVE

1. S. Freud: "Drives and their vicissitudes", *Papers on Metapsychology*, 1915.
2. "Throes of Love: The Field of the Metaphor", in TL, 277-8.
3. J. Kristeva: "Événement et révélation", *L'Infini*, 5, Winter, 1984, 5.
4. "Baudelaire, or Infinity, Perfume, and Punk", TL, 319.
5. "Throes of Love: The Field of the Metaphor", TL, 279.
6. John Lechte: "Art, Love and Melancholy in the Work of Julia Kristeva", in J. Fletcher, 1990, 24.

BIBLIOGRAPHY

Titles in English are published in London, England, unless otherwise stated. Titles in French are published in Paris, France, unless otherwise stated.

JULIA KRISTEVA

About Chinese Women, tr. A. Barrows, Boyars, 1977

Desire in Language: A Semiotic Approach to Literature and Art, ed. Leon Roudiez, tr. Thomas Gora, Alice Jardine & Leon Roudiez, Blackwell, 1982

Powers of Horror: An Essay on Abjection, tr. Leon S. Roudiez, Columbia University Press, New York, 1982

Revolution in Poetic Language, tr. Margaret Walker, Columbia University Press, New York, 1984

The Kristeva Reader, ed. Toril Moi, Blackwell, 1986

Tales of Love, tr. Leon S. Roudiez, Columbia University Press, New York 1987

In the Beginning Was Love: Psychoanalysis and Faith, tr. Arthur Goldhammer, Columbia University Press, New York, 1988

Black Sun: Depression and Melancholy, tr. L.S. Roudiez, Columbia University Press, New York, 1989

Language, The Unknown: An Initiation into Linguistics, tr. Anne M. Menke, Harvester Wheatsheaf, 1989

Strangers to Ourselves, tr. L.S. Roudiez, Harvester Wheatsheaf, 1991

The Old Man and the Wolves, Columbia University Press, New York, 1994

Julia Kristeva Interviews, ed. R. Guberman, Columbia University Press, New York, New York, 1996

Time and Sense, Columbia University Press, New York, 1998

The Crisis of the European Subject, Other Press, 2000

Intimate Revolt, Columbia University Press, New York, 2001

The Sense and Non-Sense, Columbia University Press, New York, 2001

The Portable Kristeva, ed. K. Oliver, Columbia University Press, New York, 1997/ 2002

Colette, Columbia University Press, New York, 2006

Sémétiotikè: Recherches pour une sémanalyse, Seuil, 1969

Texte du roman, Mouton, 1970

Polylogue, Seuil, 1977

La Folle Verité, Editions du Seuil, 1979

Pouvoir de l'horreur: Essai sur l'abjection, Seuil, 1980

Histoires d'amour, Denoël, 1983

Au commencement était l'amour: psychoanalyse et foi, Hachette, 1985

Soleil noir, Gallimard, 1987

Etrangers à nous-mêmes, Fayard, 1988

Les Samouraîs, Fayard, 1990

Visions Capitales, Réunion des Musées Nationaux, 1998

L'Avenir d'une révolte, Calmann-Lévy, 1998

Contre la dépression nationale, entretiens avec Ph. Petit, Textuel, 1998

Proust, Legenda, 1998

Le Génie féminin, tome I, *Hannah Arendt*, 1999, Folio, Essais, no., 432

Le Génie féminin, tome II, *Mélanie Klein*, 2000, Folio, Essais, no., 433

Le Génie féminin, tome III, *Colette*, 2002, Folio, Essais, no., 442

Au risque de la pensée, éditions de l'Aube, 2001

JULIA KRISTEVA

Micropolitique, éditions de l'Aube, 2001
Revolt She Said, Semiotext, 2002
Lettre ouverte au président de la République sur les citoyens en situation de handicap, à l'usage de ceux qui le sont et ceux qui ne le sont pas, 2003
Chroniques du temps sensible, éditions de l'Aube, 2003
La Haine et le Pardon, 2005
Seule une femme, éditions de l'Aube, 2007
Cet incroyable besoin de croire, Bayard, 2007
Thérèse mon amour, 2008

"La femme, ce n'est jamais ça", *Tel Quel*, Autumn, 1974, in E. Marks
"The Speaking Subject and Poetical Language", paper, Cambridge University, 1975
"The system and the speaking subject", in T. Sebeok, 1975
"Signifying Practice and Mode of Production", *Edinburgh '76 Magazine*, 1, 1976
"Julia Kristeva: à quoi servent les intellectuels?", interview, *Le Nouvel Observateur*, 20 June, 1977
"Un nouveau type d'intellectuel: le dissident", *Tel Quel*, 74, 1977
"Il n'y a pas de maître à language", *Nouvelle revue de psychoanalyse*, 20, Autumn, 1979
"Mémoire", *L'Infini*, 1, Winter, 1983
"Joyce, le retour d'Orphée", *L'Infini*, 8, Autumn, 1984
"Interview with Julia Kristeva", [with Perry Meisel], tr. Margaret Waller, *Partisan Review*, 51, Winter, 1984
"Julia Kristeva in conversation with Rosalind Coward", *ICA Documents*, 'Desire' issue, 1984
"Entretien avec Julia Kristeva, réalisé par Françoise Collin", *Les Cahiers du GRIF*, 32, 1985
"An Interview with Julia Kristeva", [with Edith Kurzweil], *Partisan Review*, LIII, 2, 1986
"Les abîmes de l'âme", *Magazine littéraire*, 224, August, 1987
"Jackson Pollock's Milky Way, 1912-56", *Journal of Philosophy and the Visual Arts*, 1, 1989
"A Question of Subjectivity: an interview" [with Susan Sellers], *Women's Review*, 12, 1986, in P. Rice, 1992

✤ *143*

OTHERS

Jeffner Allen & Iris Marion Young, eds. *The Thinking Muse: Feminism and Modern French Philosophy*, Indiana University Press, Bloomington, 1989

Keith Ansell-Pearson & Howard Caygill, eds. *The Fate of the New Nietzsche*, Avebury, 1993

Alison Assister. *Althusser and Feminism*, Pluto Press, 1990

—. & Avedon Carol, eds. *Bad Girls and Dirty Pictures: The Challenge to Reclaim Feminism*, Pluto Press, 1993

Margaret Attack "The Other Feminist", *Paragraph*, 8, 1986

—& Phil Powrie, eds. *Contemporary French Fiction by Women*, Manchester University Press, 1990

Lang Baker: "Irigaray contre Bataille: Locating the Feminine in Nietzsche", *Social Discourse*, 2, 1989

Francis Barker *et al*, eds. *The Politics of Theory: The Proceedings of the Essex Conference on the Psychology of Literature*, University of Essex, Colchester, 1983

Michèle Barrett & Anne Phillips, eds. *Destablizing Theory: Contemporary Feminist Debates*, Polity Press, 1992

Roland Barthes: *The Pleasure of the Text*, Hill and Wang, New York, 1975

—. *Mythologies*, Hill & Wang, New York, 1972

—. *S/Z*, Hill and Wang, New York, 1974

—. *Image, Music, Text*, tr. Stephen Heath, Fontana, 1984

Elaine Hoffman Baruch & Lucienne Serrano: *Women Analyse Women in France, England and the United States*, Harvester Wheatsheaf, 1988

S. Beardsworth. *Julia Kristeva*, State University of New York Press, NY, 2004

Ruth Behar, ed. *Women Writing Culture*, University of California Press, 1995

Ernst Behler: *Derrida – Nietzsche/ Nietzsche – Derrida*, Schöningh, Munich, 1988

Catherine Belsey: *Critical Practice*, Routledge, 1980

—*Desire: Love Stories in Western Culture*, Blackwell, 1994

Mary Berg: "Escaping the Cave: Luce Irigaray and Her Feminist Critics", in Gary Wihl & David Williams, eds. *Literature and Ethics*, McGill, Kingston, 1988

Philippa Berry & Andrew Wernick, eds. *Shadow of Spirit: Postmodernism and Religion*, Routledge, 1992

F. Bonner *et al*, eds. *Imagining Women Cultural Representations and Gender*, Polity Press, Cambridge, 1992

C.M. Bove: The Politics of Desire in Julia Kristeva", *Boundary*, 2, 12, 1984

E. Brater, ed. *Feminine Focus: The New Women Playwrights*, Oxford University Press, 1989

Teresa Brennan, ed. *Between Feminism and Psychoanalysis*, Routledge 1989

Peter Brooker, ed. *Modernism/ Postmodernism*, Longman, 1992

L. Brouwer *et al*, eds. *Beyond Limits,* University of Groningen Press, Groningen, 1990

B. Brown & P. Adams: "The feminine body and feminist politics", *M/F*, 3, 1979

Wendy Brown: "Hesitations, Postmodern Exposures", *differences*, 3, 1, 1991

David Buckingham, ed. *Reading Audiences*, Manchester University Press, 1995

Peter J. Burgard, ed. *Nietzsche and the Feminine*, University Press of Virginia, Charlottesville, 1994

Victor Burgin *et al*, eds. *Formations of Fantasy*, Methuen, 1986

Carolyn Burke: "Rethinking the maternal", in H. Eisenstein, 1980

Judith Butler: *Gender Trouble: Feminism and the Subversion of Identity*, Routledge, 1990

— & J.W. Scott, eds. *Feminists Theorise the Political*, Routledge, 1992

Colette Camelin: "La Scène de la fille dans *Illa*", *Littérature*, 67, October, 1987

Deborah Cameron, ed. *The Feminist Critique of Language: A Reader*, Routledge, 1990

Claudia Card, ed. *Adventures in Lesbian Philosophy*, Indiana University Press, 1994

Gail Chester & Julienne Dickey, ed. *Feminism and Censorship: The Current Debate*, Prism Press, Bridport, Dorset, 1988

Laura Chester, ed. *Deep Down: New Sensual Writing By Women*, Faber, 1987

Hélène Cixous. *The Newly Born Woman*, tr. Betsy Wing, Minnesota University Press, Minneapolis, 1986

—. *The Hélène Cixous Reader*, ed. Susan Sellers, Blackwell, 1994

Richard A. Cohen, ed. *Face to Face with Levinas*, SUNY Press, Albany, 1986

Alex Comfort: *I and That*, Beazley, 1979

Verena Andermatt Conley: "Julia Kristeva and the Traversal of Modern Poetic Space", *Enclitic*, 1, 1977

—. *Hélène Cixous: Writing the Feminine*, University of Nebraska Press, Lincoln, 1991

—. *Hélène Cixous*, Harvester Wheatsheaf, 1992

Diane Griffin Crowder: "Amazons and mothers? Monique Wittig, Hélène Cixous and theories of women's writing", *Contemporary Literature*, 24, Summer, 1983

Arleen Dallery: "The Politics of Writing (the) Body: *Écriture Féminine*", in A. Jaggar, 1989

Mary Daly: *Pure Lust: Elemental Feminist Philosophy*, Women's Press, 1984

G. Day & C. Bloch, eds. *Perspectives on Pornography: Sexuality in Film and Literature*, Macmillan, 1988

Christine Delphy: *The Main Enemy: A Materialist Analysis of Women's Oppression*, Women's Research and Resources Centre, 1977

Jacques Derrida: '*Speech and Phenomena' and Other Essays on Husserl's Theory of Signs*, tr. David B. Allison, Northwestern University Press, Evanton, 1973

—. *Of Grammatology*, John Hopkins University Press, Baltimore, 1976

—. *Spurs: Nietzsche's Styles*, University of Chicago Press, Chicago, 1979

—. *Writing and Difference*, University of Chicago Press, 1987

Laura Doan, ed. *The Lesbian Postmodern*, Columbia University Press, New York, 1994

Mary Ann Doane: *The Desire to Desire: The Woman's Film of the 1940's*, Macmillan, 1988

Claire Duchen: *Feminism in France From May '68 to Mitterand*, Routledge, 1986

—ed: *French Connections: Voices From the Women's Movement in France*, Hutchinson, 1987

Rachel DuPlessis: "For the Etruscans", in E. Showalter, 1986

J. Duran. *Toward a Feminist Epistemology*, Savage, Rowman & Littlefield, 1991

Andrea Dworkin: *Intercourse*, Arrow, 1988

—*Pornography: Men Possessing Women*, Women's Press, 1984

—*Letters From a War Zone*, Secker & Warburg, 1988

Mary Eagleton, ed: *Feminist Literary Theory: A Reader*, Blackwell, 1986

—. ed. *Feminist Literary Criticism*, Longman, 1991

Anthony Easthope, ed. *Contemporary Film Theory*, Longman, 1993

Hester Eisenstein & Alice Jardine, eds. *The Future of Difference*, Barnard College Women's Center, New York, 1980

—. *Contemporary Feminist Thought*, Unwin Paperbacks 1984

M. Ellman, ed. *Thinking about Women*, Virago, 1979

J. Epstein & K. Straub, eds. *Body Guards: The Cultural Politics of Gender Ambiguity*, Routledge, New York, 1991

Christine Faure: "The twilight of the goddesses, or the intellectual crisis of French feminism", *Signs*, 7, 1981

R. Felski: *Beyond Feminist Aesthetics: Feminist Literature and Social Change,* Hutchinson, 1989

Josette Féral: "China, Women and the Symbolic: An Interview with Julia Kristeva" *SubStance*, 13, 1976

—"Antigone or the irony of the tribe", *Diacritics*, Autumn, 1978

—"The Powers of Difference", in H. Eisenstein, 1980

John Fletcher & Andrew Benjamin, ed;. *Abjection, Melancholia and Love: the Work of Julia Kristeva*, Routledge, 1990

Penny Florence & Dee Reynolds, eds. *Feminist subjects, multi-media: Cultural methodologies*, Manchester University Press, 1995

Sigmund Freud: *Standard Edition of the Complete Psychological Works of Sigmund Freud*, 24 vols, ed. James Strachey, Hogarth Press, 1953-74

Diana Fuss: *Essentially Speaking*, Routledge, New York, 1989

—ed: *Inside/Out: Lesbian Theories, Gay Theories*, Routledge, 1991

Jane Gallop: *Feminism and Psychoanalysis: the daughter's seduction,* Macmillan, 1982

—. *Thinking Through the Body*, Columbia University Press, New York, 1988

Lorraine Gamman & Margaret Marshment, eds. *The Female Gaze: Women as Viewers of Popular Culture*, Women's Press, 1988

Ann Garry & Marilyn Pearsal, eds. *Women, Knowledge and Reality: explorations in feminist philosophy*, Unwin Hyman, 1989

Xavière Gauthier: "Pourquoi Sorcières?", in *Sorcières*, 1, 1976, in E. Marks, 1981

Serge Gavronsky, ed. *Toward a New Poetics: Contemporary Writing in France*, University California Press, Berkeley, 1994

Elissa D. Gelfand & Virginia Thorndike Hules: *French Feminist Criticism,* Garland, New York, 1985

Pamela Church Gibson & Roma Gibson, ed. *Dirty Looks: Women, Pornography, Power*, British Film Institute, 1993

M.A. Gillespie & T.B. Strong, eds. *Nietzsche: Explorations in Philosophy,*

Aesthetics, and Politics, University of Chicago Press, Chicago, 1988

Gayle Greene & Coppélia Kahn, eds. *Making a Difference: Feminist Literary Criticism*, Methuen, 1985

Gabriele Griffin, ed: *Outwrite: Lesbianism and Popular Culture*, Pluto Press, 1993

— . *et al*, eds. *Stirring It: Challenges For Feminism*, Taylor & Francis, 1994

Susan Griffin: *Pornography and Silence: Culture's Revenge Against Nature*, Women's Press, 1981

Morwenna Griffiths & Margaret Whitford, eds. *Feminist Perspectives in Philosophy*, Indiana University Press, Bloomington, 1988

Elizabeth Grosz: "Philosophy, Subjectivity and the Body", in C. Pateman, 1986

— "Desire, the body and recent French feminism", *Intervention*, 21-2, 1988

— *Sexual Subversions*, Allen & Unwin, 1989

— "The Body of Signification", in J. Fletcher, 1990

— "Lesbian Fetishism?", *differences*, 3, 2, 1991

— "Fetishization", in E. Wright, 1992

— "Julia Kristeva", in E. Wright, 1992

— . *Volatile Bodies,* Indiana University Press, Bloomington, 1994

— . "Refiguring Lesbian Desire", in Doan, 1994

— . *Space, Time and Perversion,* Routledge, 1995

Lynda Hart, ed. *Making a Spectacle: Feminist Essays on Contemporary Women's Theatre*, University of Michigan Press, Ann Arbor, 1989

Susan J. Hekman: *Gender and Knowledge: Elements of a Postmodern Feminism*, Polity Press, 1990

Molly Hite: "Writing – and reading – the body: female sexuality and recent feminist fiction", *Feminist Studies*, 14, 1, 1988

Sarah Lucia Hoagland & Julia Penelope, eds. *For Lesbians Only: A separatist anthology*, Onlywomen Press, 1988

Christine Holmlund: "I Love Luce: The Lesbian, Mimesis and Masquerade in Irigaray, Freud, and Mainstream Film", *New Formations*, 8, Autumn, 1989

Maggie Humm: *Feminisms: A Reader*, Harvester Wheatsheaf, 1992

— ed: *The Dictionary of Feminist Theory*, Harvester Wheatsheaf, 1995

Andreas Huyssen: *After the Great Divide: Modernism, Mass Culture, Postmodernism*, Indiana University Press, Bloomington, 1986

Luce Irigaray. *This Sex Which Is Not One*, tr. C. Porter & C. Burke, Cornell University Press, New York, 1977

— *Speculum of the Other Woman*, tr. G.C. Gill, Cornell University Press,

New York, 1985

—. *The Irigaray Reader,* ed. Margaret Whitford, Blackwell, Oxford, 1991

—*Marine Lover of Friedrich Nietzsche*, tr. G.C. Gill, Columbia University Press, New York, 1991

—*Je, tu, nous: Toward a Culture of Difference*, tr. Alison Martin, Routledge, 1993

—*An Ethics of Sexual Difference*, Athlone, 1993

—*Thinking the Difference: For a Peaceful Revolution*, Athlone Press, 1994

Mary Jacobus, ed. *Women Writing and Writing About Women*, Croom Helm, 1979

— *Reading Woman: essays in feminist criticism*, Methuen, 1986

—"Madonna: Like a Virgin, or, Freud, Kristeva, and the Case of the Missing Mother", *Oxford Literary Review*, 8, 1986

A. Jaggar & S.R. Bordo, eds. *Gender/ Body/ Knowledge: Feminist Reconstructions of Being and Knowing*, Rutgers University Press, New Brunswick, 1989

Alice Jardine. "Theories of the Feminine: Kristeva", *Enclitic*, 4, 2, 1980

—. *Gynesis,* Cornell University Press, New York, 1985

—. "Opaque Texts", in N. Miller, 1986

—& Anne M. Menke: "Exploding the Issue: 'French' 'Women' 'Writers' and 'the Canon'?", *Yale French Studies*, 75, 1988

—& Anne Menke, eds. *Shifting Scenes: interviews on women, writing and politics in post '68 France*, Columbia University Press, New York, 1991

Karla Jay, ed. *Lesbian Erotics,* New York University Press, 1995

Ann Rosalind Jones: "Julia Kristeva on femininity: the limits of a semiotic politics", *Feminist Review*, 18, Winter, 1984

—"Writing the Body: Toward an Understanding of L'Écriture féminine", in E. Showalter, 1986

Jordan Jones: "Renewing the Dance: René Daumal, the Surrealism of the Bardo, and Shamanic Poetry", *Heaven Bone*, 11, Spring, 1994

C.G. Jung: *Memories, Dreams, Reflections*, Collins, 1967

Laura Kipnis: "Feminism: the Political Conscience of Postmodernism?", in P. Brooker, 1992

Vivian Kogan: "I Want Vulva? Hélène Cixous and the Poetics of the Body", *L'Esprit créateur*, 25, 2, Summer, 1985

David Farrell Krell: *Postponement: Women, Sensuality, and Death in Nietzsche*, Indiana University Press, Bloomington, 1986

—& David Woods: *Exceedingly Nietzsche: Aspects of Contemporary Nietzsche-Interpretation*, Routledge, 1988

A. & M. Kroker, eds. *The Hysterical Male: New Feminist Theory*, St Martin's Press, New York, NY, 1991

Annette Kuhn: *Women's Pictures: Feminism and the Cinema*, Routledge & Kegan Paul, 1982

Jacques Lacan and the École Freudienne: *Feminine Sexuality*, ed. Juliet Mitchell and Jacqueline Rose, Macmillan, 1988

— *Écrits: A Selection*, tr. Alan Sheridan, Tavistock, 1977

D. Landry & G. MacLean. *Unbearable Weight*, Blackwell, Oxford, 1993

Rob Lapsley & Michael Westlake: "From *Casablanca* to *Pretty Woman*: the Politics of Romance", *Screen*, 33, 1, Spring, 1992

Teresa de Laurentis, ed. *Feminist Studies/ Critical Studies*, Macmillan, 1988

John Lechte: *Julia Kristeva*, Routledge, 1990 (a)

— "Art, Love, and Melancholy in the Work of Julia Kristeva", in J. Fletcher, 1990 (b)

— *The Critical Julia Kristeva Reader*, Edinburgh University Press, Edinburgh, 2003

S. Lefanu: *In the Chinks of the World Machine: Feminism and Science Fiction*, Women's Press, 1988

Philip Lewis: "Revolutionary Semiotics", *Diacritics*, 4, 3, Autumn, 1974

Cecile Lindsay: "Body Language: French Feminist Utopias", *The French Review*, 60, 1, October, 1986

Juliet Flower MacCannell, ed. *The Other Perspective in Gender and Culture: Rewriting Women and the Symbolic*, Columbia University Press, New York, 1990

Elaine Marks & Isabelle de Courtivron, eds. *New French Feminisms: an Anthology*, Harvester Wheatsheaf, 1981

M. Maynard & J. Purvis, eds. *Researching Woman's Lives*, Taylor & Francis, 1994

Geraldine Meaney: *(Un)Like Subjects: Women, Theory, Fiction*, Routledge, 1993

Elaine Millard: "French Feminisms", in S. Mills, 1989

N.K. Miller, ed. *The Poetics of Gender*, Columbia University Press, New York, 1986

Kate Millett: *Sexual Politics*, Doubleday, Garden City, 1970

Sara Mills *et al*, eds. *Feminist Readings/ Feminists Reading*, University Press of Virginia, Charlottesville, 1989

—. ed. *Gendering the Reader*, Harvester Wheatsheaf, 1993

Toril Moi: *Sexual/ Textual Politics: Feminist Literary Theory*, Routledge,

1988

—ed: *French Feminist Thought*, Blackwell, 1988

Jan Montefiore: *Feminism and Poetry: Language, Experience, Identity in Women's Writing*, Pandora, 1987

Moira Monteith, ed. *Women's Writing: A Challenge to Theory*, Harvester Press, Brighton, Sussex, 1986

Raoul Mortley: *French Philosophers in Conversation: Derrida, Irigaray, Levinas, Le Doeuff, Schneider, Serres*, Routledge, 1991

Laura Mulvey: *Visual and Other Pleasures*, Macmillan, 1989

Sally Munt, ed. *New Lesbian Criticism: Literary and Cultural Readings*, Harvester Wheatsheaf, 1992

Lynda Nead: *Female Nude: Art, Obscenity and Sexuality*, Routledge, 1992

Friedrich Nietzsche: *A Nietzsche Reader*, ed. R.J. Hollingdale, Penguin, 1977

Andrea Nye: "Preparing the way for a feminist praxis", *Hypatia*, 1, 1986

—. "The woman clothed with the sun: Julia Kristeva and the escape from/to language", *Signs*, 12, 4, 1987

—. "The voice of the serpent: French feminism and the philosophy of language", in A. Garry, 1989

D.T. O'Hara, ed. *Why Nietzsche Now?*, Indiana University Press, Bloomington, 1985

Bat-Ami Bar On, ed. *Modern Engendering: Critical Feminist Readings in Modern Western Philosophy*, SUNY Press, Albany, 1994

Sherry B. Ortner: "Is Female to Male as Nature is to Culture", in M. Evans, ed. *The Woman Question*, Fontana, 1982

Claire Pajaczkowska: "Introduction to Kristeva", *m/f*, 5 & 6, 1981

Carole Pateman & Elizabeth Grosz, eds. *Feminist Challenges*, Allen & Unwin, Sydney, 1986

Michael Payne: *Reading Theory: An Introduction to Lacan, Derrida, and Kristeva*, Blackwell, 1993

Monique Plaza: ""Phallomorphic power" and the psychology of "woman"", *Ideology and Consciousness*, 4, 1978

E.D. Pribram, ed. *Female Spectators: Looking At Film and TV*, Verso, 1988

Leslie Rabine: "Julia Kristeva: Semiotics and Women", *Pacific Coast Philology*, 12, 1977

—. "Écriture Féminine as Metaphor", *Cultural Critique*, 8, Winter, 1987/8

Jean Radford: "Coming to terms: Dorothy Richardson, Modernism and Women", *News from Nowhere*, 7, Winter, 1989

H.L. Radtke & H.J. Stam, eds. *Gender and Power*, Sage, 1994

Janice Radway: *Reading the Romance: Feminism and the Representation of Women in Popular Culture*, University of North Carolina Press, Chapel Hill, 1984

J.L. Reich: "Genderfuck: The Law of the Dildo", *Discourse: Journal of Theoretical Studies in Media and Culture*, 15, 1, 1992

Philip Rice & Patricia Waugh, eds. *Modern Literary Theory: A Reader*, Arnold, 1992

Adrienne Rich: *Of Woman Born: Motherhood as Experience and Institution*, Virago, 1977

—. *Blood, Bread and Poetry*, Virago, 1980

Michèle Richman: "Sex and Signs: The Language of French Feminist Criticism", *Language and Style*, 13, 4, Autumn, 1980

Jeanne Addison Roberts: *The Shakespearean Wild: Geography, Genus and Gender*, University of Nebraska Press, Lincoln, Nebraska, 1991

Jacqueline Rose: *Sexuality in the Field of Vision*, Verso, 1986

Françoise van Rossum-Guyon & Myriam Diaz-Diocaretz, eds. *Hélène Cixous: chemins d'une écriture*, Rodopi, Amsterdam, 1990

Tilde Sankovitch: *French Women Writers and the Book: Myths of Access and Desire*, Syracuse University Press, Syracuse, 1988

Eva Martin Sartori & Dorothy Wynne Zimmerman, eds. *French Women Writers*, University Press, Lincoln, 1994

Janet Sayers: *Biological Politics*, Tavistock, 1982

Naomi Schor: *Breaking the Chain: Women, Theory and French Realist Fiction*, New York, 1985

—& Elizabeth Weed, eds. *Differences: More Gender Trouble: Feminism Meets Queer Theory*, Indiana University Press, 6, 2-3, Summer, 1994

Thomas A. Sebeok, ed. *The Tell-Tale Sign: A survey of semiotics*, Peter de Ridder Press, Lisse, Netherlands, 1975

Susan Sellers, ed. *Writing Differences: Readings From the Seminar of Hélène Cixous*, Open University Press, 1988

—ed: *Delighting the Heart: A Notebook by Women Writers*, Women's Press, 1989

—*Language and Sexual Difference: Feminist Writing in France*, Macmillan, 1991

—ed: *Feminist Criticism: Theory and Practice*, Harvester Wheatsheaf, 1991

Morag Shiach: *Hélène Cixous: A Politics of Writing*, Routledge, 1991

Elaine Showalter, ed. *The New Feminist Criticism*, Virago, 1986

Kaja Silverman: *The Acoustic Mirror: The Female Voice in Psychoanalysis and Cinema*, Indiana University Press, Bloomington, 1988

Dale Spender: *The Writing or the Sex? why you don't have to read women's writing to know it's no good*, Pergamon Press, New York, 1989

Gayatri Chakravorty Spivak: "French feminism in an international frame", *Yale French Studies*, 62, 1981

—. *The Post-Colonial Critic: Interviews, Strategies, Dialogues*, ed. Sarah Harasym, Routledge, 1990

George Stambolian & Elaine Marks, eds. *Homosexuality and French Literature: Cultural Contexts/ Critical Texts*, Cornell University Press, Ithaca, 1979

Donna C. Stanton: "Difference on Trial: Critique of the Maternal Metaphor in Cixous, Irigaray, and Kristeva", in N. Miller, 1986

Crista Stevens: "Hélène Cixous: Portraying the Feminine", in L. Brouwer, 1990

Judith Still & Michael Worton, eds. *Textuality and Sexuality: Reading Theories and Practices*, Manchester University Press, 1993

Judith Stone: "The horror of power: a critique of 'Kristeva'", in F. Barker, 1983

John Storey, ed. *Cultural Theory and Popular Culture*, Harvester Wheatsheaf, 1994

Susan Rubin Suleiman, ed. *Subversive Intent: Gender, Politics and the Avant-Garde*, Harvard University Press, 1990

— *Risking Who One Is*, MIT Press, 1995

Helene Volat-Shapiro: "Julia Kristeva: A Bibliography of Her Writings", *Bulletin of Bibliography*, 45, 1, 1988

Helene Wenzel. "The text and body/ politics: an appreciation of Monique Wittig's writings in context", *Feminist Studies*, 7, 1981

Allon White: "L'eclatement du sujet: The Theoretical Work of Julia Kristeva", paper, University of Birmingham, 1977

— '*L'éclatement du sujet: The Theoretical Work of Julia Kristeva*, Centre for Contemporary Studies, University of Birmingham, 1977

Margaret Whitford: *Luce Irigaray: Philosophy in the Feminine*, Routledge, 1991

Helen Wilcox *et al*, eds. *The Body and the Text: Hélène Cixous, Reading and Teaching*, Harvester Wheatsheaf, 1990

S. Wilkinson & C. Kitzinger, eds. *Heterosexuality: A Feminism and Psychology Reader*, Sage, 1993

Linda Ruth Williams: *Critical Desire: Psychoanalysis and the Literary Subject*, Arnold, 1995

— *Sex in the Head*, Harvester Wheatsheaf, 1995

Monique Wittig: *Les Guerillères*, tr. David Le Vay, Viking, New York 1971

—. "One is Not Born A Woman", *Feminist Issues*, 1, 3, Winter 1981

—. "Mark of Gender", *Feminist Issues*, 5, 2, 1985

—. *The Lesbian Body*, tr. David Le Vay, Beacon Press, Boston 1986

—. *The Straight Mind*, Beacon Press, Boston 1992

Elizabeth Wright, ed. *Feminism and Psychoanalysis: A Critical Dictionary*, Blackwell, 1992

Evelyn Zepp: "The Criticism of Julia Kristeva: A New Mode of Critical Thought", *Romanic Review*, 73, 1982

Peter Zima, ed. *Semiotics and Dialectics: Ideology and the Text*, Benjamins, Amsterdam, 1981

Jack Zipes: *Don't Bet on the Prince: Contemporary Feminist Fairy Tales in North America and England*, Methuen, New York, 1986

WEBSITES

irigaray.org
kristeva.fr
kristevacircle.org

CRESCENT MOON PUBLISHING

ARTS, PAINTING, SCULPTURE

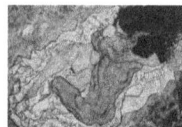

LITERATURE

J.R.R. Tolkien: The Books, The Films, The Whole Cultural Phenomenon
J.R.R. Tolkien: Pocket Guide
Tolkien's Heroic Quest
The *Earthsea* Books of Ursula Le Guin
Beauties, Beasts and Enchantment: Classic French Fairy Tales
German Popular Stories by the Brothers Grimm
Philip Pullman and *His Dark Materials*
Sexing Hardy: Thomas Hardy and Feminism
Thomas Hardy's *Tess of the d'Urbervilles*
Thomas Hardy's *Jude the Obscure*
Thomas Hardy: The Tragic Novels
Love and Tragedy: Thomas Hardy
The Poetry of Landscape in Hardy
Wessex Revisited: Thomas Hardy and John Cowper Powys
Wolfgang Iser: Essays and Interviews
Petrarch, Dante and the Troubadours
Maurice Sendak and the Art of Children's Book Illustration
Andrea Dworkin
Cixous, Irigaray, Kristeva: The *Jouissance* of French Feminism
Julia Kristeva: Art, Love, Melancholy, Philosophy, Semiotics and Psychoanalysis
Hélène Cixous I Love You: The *Jouissance* of Writing
Luce Irigaray: Lips, Kissing, and the Politics of Sexual Difference
Peter Redgrove: Here Comes the Flood
Peter Redgrove: Sex-Magic-Poetry-Cornwall
Lawrence Durrell: Between Love and Death, East and West
Love, Culture & Poetry: Lawrence Durrell
Cavafy: Anatomy of a Soul
German Romantic Poetry: Goethe, Novalis, Heine, Hölderlin
Feminism and Shakespeare
Shakespeare: Love, Poetry & Magic
The Passion of D.H. Lawrence
D.H. Lawrence: Symbolic Landscapes
D.H. Lawrence: Infinite Sensual Violence
Rimbaud: Arthur Rimbaud and the Magic of Poetry
The Ecstasies of John Cowper Powys
Sensualism and Mythology: The Wessex Novels of John Cowper Powys
Amorous Life: John Cowper Powys and the Manifestation of Affectivity (H.W. Fawkner)
Postmodern Powys: New Essays on John Cowper Powys (Joe Boulter)
Rethinking Powys: Critical Essays on John Cowper Powys
Paul Bowles & Bernardo Bertolucci
Rainer Maria Rilke
Joseph Conrad: *Heart of Darkness*
In the Dim Void: Samuel Beckett
Samuel Beckett Goes into the Silence
André Gide: Fiction and Fervour
Jackie Collins and the Blockbuster Novel
Blinded By Her Light: The Love-Poetry of Robert Graves
The Passion of Colours: Travels In Mediterranean Lands
Poetic Forms

POETRY

Ursula Le Guin: Walking In Cornwall
Peter Redgrove: Here Comes The Flood
Peter Redgrove: Sex-Magic-Poetry-Cornwall
Dante: Selections From the Vita Nuova
Petrarch, Dante and the Troubadours
William Shakespeare: Sonnets
William Shakespeare: Complete Poems
Blinded By Her Light: The Love-Poetry of Robert Graves
Emily Dickinson: Selected Poems
Emily Brontë: Poems
Thomas Hardy: Selected Poems
Percy Bysshe Shelley: Poems
John Keats: Selected Poems
Joh n Keats: Poems of 1820
D.H. Lawrence: Selected Poems
Edmund Spenser: Poems
Edmund Spenser: Amoretti
John Donne: Poems
Henry Vaughan: Poems
Sir Thomas Wyatt: Poems
Robert Herrick: Selected Poems
Rilke: Space, Essence and Angels in the Poetry of Rainer Maria Rilke
Rainer Maria Rilke: Selected Poems
Friedrich Hölderlin: Selected Poems
Arseny Tarkovsky: Selected Poems
Arthur Rimbaud: Selected Poems
Arthur Rimbaud: A Season in Hell
Arthur Rimbaud and the Magic of Poetry
Novalis: Hymns To the Night
German Romantic Poetry
Paul Verlaine: Selected Poems
Elizaethan Sonnet Cycles
D.J. Enright: By-Blows
Jeremy Reed: Brigitte's Blue Heart
Jeremy Reed: Claudia Schiffer's Red Shoes
Gorgeous Little Orpheus
Radiance: New Poems
Crescent Moon Book of Nature Poetry
Crescent Moon Book of Love Poetry
Crescent Moon Book of Mystical Poetry
Crescent Moon Book of Elizabethan Love Poetry
Crescent Moon Book of Metaphysical Poetry
Crescent Moon Book of Romantic Poetry
Pagan America: New American Poetry

MEDIA, CINEMA, FEMINISM and CULTURAL STUDIES

J.R.R. Tolkien: The Books, The Films, The Whole Cultural Phenomenon
J.R.R. Tolkien: Pocket Guide
The *Lord of the Rings* Movies: Pocket Guide
The Cinema of Hayao Miyazaki
Hayao Miyazaki: *Princess Mononoke*: Pocket Movie Guide
Hayao Miyazaki: *Spirited Away*: Pocket Movie Guide
Tim Burton
Ken Russell
Ken Russell: *Tommy*: Pocket Movie Guide
The Ghost Dance: The Origins of Religion
The Peyote Cult
Cixous, Irigaray, Kristeva: The *Jouissance* of French Feminism
Julia Kristeva: Art, Love, Melancholy, Philosophy, Semiotics and Psychoanalysis
Luce Irigaray: Lips, Kissing, and the Politics of Sexual Difference
Hélene Cixous I Love You: The *Jouissance* of Writing
Andrea Dworkin
'Cosmo Woman': The World of Women's Magazines
Women in Pop Music
Discovering the Goddess (Geoffrey Ashe)
The Poetry of Cinema
The Sacred Cinema of Andrei Tarkovsky
Andrei Tarkovsky: Pocket Guide
Andrei Tarkovsky: *Mirror*: Pocket Movie Guide
Andrei Tarkovsky: *The Sacrifice*: Pocket Movie Guide
Walerian Borowczyk: Cinema of Erotic Dreams
Jean-Luc Godard: The Passion of Cinema
Jean-Luc Godard: *Hail Mary*: Pocket Movie Guide
Jean-Luc Godard: *Contempt*: Pocket Movie Guide
Jean-Luc Godard: *Pierrot le Fou*: Pocket Movie Guide
John Hughes and Eighties Cinema
Ferris Bueller's Day Off: Pocket Movie Guide
Jean-Luc Godard: Pocket Guide
The Cinema of Richard Linklater
Liv Tyler: Star In Ascendance
Blade Runner and the Films of Philip K. Dick
Paul Bowles and Bernardo Bertolucci
Media Hell: Radio, TV and the Press
An Open Letter to the BBC
Detonation Britain: Nuclear War in the UK
Feminism and Shakespeare
Wild Zones: Pornography, Art and Feminism
Sex in Art: Pornography and Pleasure in Painting and Sculpture
Sexing Hardy: Thomas Hardy and Feminism

In my view *The Light Eternal* is among the very best of all the material I read on Turner. (Douglas Graham, director of the Turner Museum, Denver, Colorado)

The Light Eternal is a model monograph, an exemplary job. The subject matter of the book is beautifully organised and dead on beam. (Lawrence Durrell)

It is amazing for me to see my work treated with such passion and respect. (Andrea Dworkin)

CRESCENT MOON PUBLISHING
P.O. Box 1312, Maidstone, Kent, ME14 5XU, Great Britain. www.crmoon.com

www.ingramcontent.com/pod-product-compliance
Lightning Source LLC
Chambersburg PA
CBHW031435270326
41930CB00007B/714